Black Humor Fiction of the Sixties

MAX F. SCHULZ

Black Humor Fiction of the Sixties

A Pluralistic Definition of Man and His World

OHIO UNIVERSITY PRESS / Athens, Ohio

6/1973
Eng.

© 1973 by Max F. Schulz
All Rights Reserved
Library of Congress Catalog Number: 72–85538
ISBN 8214-0125-4
Printed in the United States of America by Heritage Printers
Design by Hal Stevens

For MURIEL and ALISON, GAVIN, and EVAN, who continued wisely to grow separately as well as concurrently with this book.

Acknowledgments

Permission to quote from the works of the writers discussed in this book has been kindly granted as follows: From *Lost in the Funhouse* by John Barth, copyright © 1963, 1966, 1968, 1969 by John Barth. Reprinted by permission of Doubleday & Company, Inc. From *The Sot-Weed Factor* by John Barth, copyright © 1960 by John Barth. Reprinted by permission of Doubleday & Company, Inc.

From *Labyrinths* by Jorge Luis Borges, copyright © 1962, 1964 by New Directions Publishing Corporation. Reprinted by courtesy of New Directions Publishing Corporation. From *Journey to the End of the Night* by Louis-Ferdinand Céline, copyright 1934 by Louis-Ferdinand Céline. Reprinted by courtesy of New Directions Publishing Corporation. From *The Universal Baseball Association, Inc., J. Henry Waugh, Prop.*, copyright © 1968 by Robert Coover. Reprinted by courtesy of Random House, Inc.

From *V.* by Thomas Pynchon, copyright © 1961, 1963 by Thomas Pynchon. Reprinted by courtesy of J.B. Lippincott Company. From *The Crying of Lot 49* by Thomas Pynchon, copyright © 1966, 1965 by Thomas Pynchon. Reprinted by courtesy of J.B. Lippincott Company.

From *God Bless You, Mr. Rosewater* by Kurt Vonnegut, Jr., copyright © 1965 by Kurt Vonnegut, Jr. Reprinted by permission of Seymour Lawrence Books published by Delacorte Press. From *Cat's Cradle* by Kurt Vonnegut, Jr., copyright © 1963 by Kurt Vonnegut, Jr. Reprinted by courtesy of Seymour Lawrence Books published by Delacorte Press. From *Mother Night* by Kurt Vonnegut, Jr., copyright © 1961, 1966 by Kurt Vonnegut, Jr. Reprinted by courtesy of Seymour Lawrence Books published by Delacorte Press.

ACKNOWLEDGMENTS

From *Slaughterhouse-Five* by Kurt Vonnegut, Jr., copyright ©
1969 by Kurt Vonnegut, Jr. Reprinted by courtesy of Seymour
Lawrence Books published by Delacorte Press.

From *The Wig* by Charles Wright, copyright © 1966 by Charles
Wright. Reprinted with the permission of Farrar, Straus & Giroux,
Inc.

From *Stern* by Bruce Jay Friedman, copyright © 1962 by Bruce
Jay Friedman. Reprinted by permission of Simon and Schuster,
Inc. From *A Mother's Kisses* by Bruce Jay Friedman, copyright ©
1964 by Bruce Jay Friedman. Reprinted by permission of Simon
and Schuster, Inc. From *Catch-22* by Joseph Heller, copyright ©
1955 by Joseph Heller. Reprinted by permission of Simon and
Schuster, Inc.

Preface

The term Black Humor appears to have caught on among readers and critics as a convenient handle for referring to a divergent body of literature produced in the 1960's and still being produced. The rub is that the vagueness of the tag allows it to be bandied about, applied to writers and literature whose "blackness" or "humor" seems all that recommends them, and substituted for allied but not similar modes of discourse. The sick humor of standup comics and comedians and the gallows humor of popular culture are confused with Black Humor, indeed, identified in many minds as its principal quality. The grotesque (which has an honorable history as a critical term for the bizarre combination of natural and unnatural forms) is used interchangeably with it. Not unsurprisingly, one finds writers as dissimilar as Flannery O'Connor and Laurence Sterne lumped together as Black Humorists—neither of whom deserves being lodged so indiscriminately with strange bedfellows. Given the widespread recognition in the past five years of Black Humor as a significant body of literature and given the diffuse adoption of it as a critical term, the attempt at a careful scrutiny of its underlying assumptions is overdue. This study hopefully begins the establishment of guidelines preliminary to our coming to terms with the cultural and literary achievement represented by the Black Humor fiction of the sixties.

My primary aim then is definition, not explication. Hence, when I discuss John Barth and Leonard Cohen principally in relation to a metaphysics of multiplicity, Kurt Vonnegut in relation to his unconfirmed theses, Jorge Luis Borges, Thomas Pynchon, Thomas Berger, and Robert Coover in relation to parody, and Bruce Jay Friedman and Charles Wright in relation to their conformist heroes,

I do not mean to imply that any one category exhausts the characteristics of each novelist. (Nor for that matter do I mean to suggest that these writers are the only Black Humorists. Some works of Günter Grass and Vladimir Nabokov, especially their novels *The Tin Drum* and *Lolita*, clearly belong with the others, and I have taken note of this fact in my remarks. Convenience of exposition, however, prompted me not to present at length any part of my definition of Black Humor in terms of them.) I would like to believe that the multi-stranded definition of Black Humor I have formulated here describes in varying degree all the novels I have cited as instances of the "genre," that *The Sot-Weed Factor*, for example, is not just pluralistic, but at once self-negating, parodic, and conformist as well in its model of the world. For critical convenience only I have restricted my discussion and illustration of each point of the definition to one or two novels. To have tested every Black Humor novel against each part of the definition would have been cumbersome and laborious. I leave this ultimate confirmation to the reader.

One final observation. I have shied away from the "humor" in Black Humor. Most efforts to come to terms with the comic over the past two thousand years have drifted into the shallows of laughter and foundered on the submerged rocks of psychology's attempts to explain why we chuckle. Hence my timidity. Secondly, to give equal value to humor in any consideration of this literature is possibly to let oneself be trapped by a term that came into being somewhat capriciously and may not accurately describe that literature. Rather than be guided by the words in the phrase Black Humor, I have tried to let the fiction itself lead me to general concepts. Consequently, where I allude to the comic I have in mind the Black Humor concept of the cosmic labyrinth, which is more ironic than rib-tickling in its inferences about man's pitifully inadequate efforts to comprehend (in Borges's words in "The Library of Babel") the "divine disorder" of the cosmos. A paradigm of this "comic" situation is presented in Borges's story "Averroes' Search" in which Averroes, a twelfth-century Spanish Arab "closed within the orb of Islam," attempts in a commentary on Aristotle to comprehend tragedy and comedy and "to imagine what a drama is without ever having suspected what a theater is." The absurdity of man's blind

compulsion to put boundaries on the illimitable unknown, so power-
fully illustrated in William Blake's frontispiece to *Europe* of Urizen
"The Ancient of Days" trying to set limits to the cosmos with a
puny pair of dividers, provides us with the wry context of Black
Humor.

I have been testing these definitions in a course in Black Humor
taught with some regularity for five years now. To all students in
those classes at the University of Southern California and the State
University of New York at Stony Brook, thank you for many chal-
lenging hours of exploration and discovery. Your healthy skepticism about Black Humor fiction continually returned me to its maze
in the hope of extending my map of its construct of the world. For
readers who may not have dipped as intensely into Black Humor
fiction as these students, I have appended summaries of the novels
discussed at length.

The efforts of the secretaries of the English Department at the
University of Southern California also deserve my gratitude. Marie
Buboltz, Marge Peppers, Evie Warshawski, Frances Demmon, and
Kathy Richards have aided me in the preparation of this book
beyond the performance of their normal duties.

Through the years my wife has displayed marvelous forbearance
and continuing interest in whatever book of mine was on the work-
table. I can only wonder with gratitude at my good fortune.

Portions of this book have appeared in *College English* (some
pages of ch. 5), in *Critique* (ch. 3), and in *The Southern Review*
(parts of chs. 1 and 2), who have generously granted permission to
reprint this material, much of it in modified form.

Contents

Black Humor Fiction of the Sixties

I

TOWARDS A DEFINITION
OF BLACK HUMOR

Conrad Knickerbocker is its theoretician, Bruce Jay Friedman its field commander. Yet neither they nor their fellow partisans can agree on a common article of faith or theatre of operations. Black Humor is a movement without unity, a group of guerrillas who huddle around the same campfire only because they know that they are in Indian territory. Even though they grudgingly concur about the enemy, they anarchistically refuse to coordinate their attack. Desperate men, they have abandoned not only the safety of received opinions but have also left to the news media the advance positions of satirical shock treatment, charging instead the exposed flanks of undiscovered lands "somewhere out beyond satire," which require "a new set of filters" to be seen.[1]

The irony is that Friedman inadvertently gave literary respectability and philosophical cohesion to the group, when he patched together thirteen pieces (short stories and excerpts from novels, including one of his own, "Black Angels") for Bantam Books in 1965 and nonchalantly entitled them *Black Humor*. The other twelve writers on whom he had perpetrated this travesty were Terry Southern, John Rechy, J. P. Donleavy, Edward Albee, Charles Simmons, Louis-Ferdinand Céline, James Purdy, Joseph Heller, Thomas Pynchon, Vladimir Nabokov, Conrad Knickerbocker, and John Barth. The venture was an exercise in book making. Friedman's novels had had good critical reception but modest sales; he had a living to earn, a family to support. Much to his surprise he found himself tarred with his own black label. Dumbfounded, like one of his fictional characters, to learn that someone was indeed listening, he now regrets his part in this bit of carpentry for the trade. The tag has been applied to his own fiction until he winces when he hears the words. "What I ended up with was 13 separate writers with completely private and unique visions," he admitted with ingratiating candor as early as his foreword to the collection, "who in so many ways have nothing at all to do with one another and would not know or perhaps even understand one another's work if they tripped over it."[2]

Despite Friedman's protestations and a recent effort to describe his play *Scuba Duba* with the more critically usable phrase "tense comedy," the Black Humor tag seems to have stuck. If, however, the term is to have any critical usefulness, aside from an opaque impressionistic meaning, it must be more clearly defined than hitherto. For as a term Black Humor *is* vague. It fails to distinguish among the genres. It fails to differentiate the contemporary movement from the many instances in the past of similar literary reactions to human experience. It fails to focus the means (plot, character, thought, and diction) and the end (effect on reader: laughter, tears, etc.) of literary expression, as Friedman's alternative "tense comedy" attempts more successfully to do. Indeed, Black Humor needs a definition that will be not only inclusive but exclusive.

Although several attempts have been made to define Black Humor, the results have been elusive and chimerical. (1) Despairing of any substantive formula, Friedman opts for a mystery that has been around as long as the human mind has had an iconoclastic itch to peel back disguises and to probe "thoughts no one else cares to think."[3] (2) Robert Scholes[4] tries to channel Friedman's all-out purchase on history by shifting to formalist concerns and identifying Black Humor with the recurrent intellectual reaction of artists to the limitations of realism. As with the painterly aims of some modern artists, Black Humorists, he believes, are absorbed by the possibilities of playful and artful construction. They are master fabulators in the tradition of the Romance and its baroque configurations. Like Plato's "all-in-one," unfortunately, Scholes' "fabulation" becomes in practice a nondiscriminating standard, subsuming in its alembic all "artful contrivance," for is not the artist by nature

4

a maker of patterns? Are not the stark fables of Isaac Bashevis Singer as contrived as the mannered convolutions of Vladimir Nabokov? Surely Scholes' already disparate group of fabulators, ranging from Lawrence Durrell to John Hawkes, could not deny membership to the master fabulator—and ironist—Henry James. *Hic reductio ad absurdum!* If, on the other hand, Scholes sees this fabulation as a game to be enjoyed in part for its own sake, a decadence appreciated by a developed taste for the sophisticated, the artful—as his emphasis on Nabokov and Barth as arch-fabulators would suggest—then the moral position of a Henry James or the social gesture of a Bruce Jay Friedman, a Louis-Ferdinand Céline, a Terry Southern, or a Kurt Vonnegut becomes an important distinction. This is not to deny that Nabokov and Barth have their serious themes, or that Friedman has his aestheticism, but to suggest that the ways Nabokov and Barth handle their subjects loom larger in their calculations than the stylisms of Friedman loom in his. The verbal conundrums of Nabokov and Barth in any final analysis would appear more the stance of the aesthete than the verbal uniqueness of Friedman. And Scholes' definition would seem inevitably to polarize the practitioners of Black Humor into at least two groups distinguishable by the formalist means they employ. (3) Conrad Knickerbocker in his groundbreaking essay[5] diminishes the Black Humorist to *poète maudit*, a scorpion to the status quo, so full of the poison of self-loathing for the "specially tailored, ready-to-wear identities" given to us by TV, movies, the press, universities, the government, the military, medicine, and business, that he mortally stings himself, pricking the surrogate skin of society.[6]

We unnecessarily compound the problem of determining what Black Humor is when we try, like Scholes, to see it as a universal attitude of mind, periodically emerging in the history of literature. Such a *via media* leads to an impasse not unlike that reached by those critics who make romanticism and classicism out to be constant modes of apprehending human experience. More limiting, certainly, but more useful in the long run is to recognize that Black Humor is a phenomenon of the 1960's, comprising a group of writers who share a viewpoint and an aesthetics for pacing off the boundaries of a nuclear-technological world intrinsically without confinement. Equally useful is to discriminate Black Humor from

5

the oral techniques of sick humor and from the dramatic conventions of the theater of the absurd, even though it shares with these modes of expression some of the same assumptions about our century. In this respect, Hamlin Hill's essay,[7] whose subject is the confrontation of humorist and audience, analyzes the technique of such stand-up comedians as Mort Sahl, Mike Nichols, and Lennie Bruce, and the sick humor of Jules Feiffer and Paul Krassner, rather than the literary form of Black Humor; hence it somewhat unwittingly is of help in discriminating sick humor from Black Humor but not in defining Black Humor which was purportedly its intention. And *Catch-22*, widely heralded as a Black Humor novel, actually derives as much from absurdist theater as from Black Humor fictional strategies. Written in the late forties and early fifties (and published in 1955), its disregard of time and space, repetitiveness of speeches, stichomythia of commonplaces, and exercises in disproportion (that is, the substitution of the trivial as vehicle for and purveyor of the serious), link it more to the plays of Ionesco and Beckett, which cry out against a complex world, than to the elegant fictional structures of Barth, Borges, Grass, Nabokov, and Pynchon. A similar transitional work is Donleavy's *The Ginger Man* (also published in 1955), which displays its Angry Young Man genesis as much as anticipates the Black Humor stance.

The possibility that Black Humor differs in its view of man from existentialism is less easy to determine. Yet I think that an effort to discriminate between the two should be made. Basically, both posit an absurd world devoid of intrinsic values, with a resultant tension between individual and universe. The existentialist, however, retains implicitly a respect for the self. Although existence precedes being, to exist is to act (even for Beckett's almost immobile characters) and to act is to assert the self. The negation of many possibilities in favor of one choice of action thus becomes an heroic primal assent to life, as in Camus' portrait of Sisyphus. More often than not with the French existentialists action leads to cosmic despair rather than to joyous wholeness of being. Nevertheless the realization of self, as with Meursault in Camus' *The Stranger*, Moses in Bellow's *Herzog*, and Rojack in Mailer's *An American Dream*, is potentially present in the act of overcoming the negation of life by

6

way of the assertion of self. Thus, while one finds in existentialism a rejection of suprapersonal law, dogma, and social order, one finds retained a confidence in the dignity and ordering capacity of the individual.

With Black Humor, choice poses the primary difficulty. This is the consequence of a shift in perspective from the self and its ability to create a moral ambience through an act to emphasis on all the moving forces of life which converge collectively upon the individual. But to affirm all possible forces in the likelihood that an act can be self creating is to deliver oneself up to skepticism that the self is anything but chimerical. Such is the plight of Barth's heroes. Yet this refusal to confirm either a suprapersonal or a personal order does not leave the Black Humorist despairing. He remains dissociated, hanging loose (or as has been suggested about Friedman "hanging by his thumbs"),[8] cooly presenting individual efforts to realize oneself in relation to the outer world, with the focus less on the individual than on the world of experiences, less on the agony of struggle to realize self than on the bewildering trackless choices that face the individual.

Nor are its grotesqueries heirs to those of Surrealism. The latter assumes the validity of the human consciousness in its reliance on the processes of dreaming for its substance. If the subconscious mind includes a certain amount of internal disorder, this is realized aesthetically in the techniques of Surrealism, as well as in those of expressionism and stream-of-consciousness. Contrariwise, external disorder, meaningless social disorder, is codified as "absurdity" in existentialist fiction.[9] And here Black Humor finds its logical home.

Divergence from traditional comedy and satire further characterizes Black Humor. New Comedy, according to Northrop Frye's "The Argument of Comedy,"[10] always worked toward a reconciliation of the individual with society. Either the normal individual was freed from the bonds of an arbitrary humor society, or a normal society was rescued from the whims imposed by humor individuals. As might be suspected, Frye finds lurking beneath this realignment of social forces the yearly triumph of spring over winter. He sees the victory of normality over abnormality as a formalized celebration of the archetypal pattern of death and resurrection. In the marriage of the young hero, in his triumph over the old lecher (*senex*), in the freeing of the slave, New Comedy rehearsed the victory of life over death.

Black Humor stops short of any such victory. It enacts no individual release or social reconciliation; it often moves toward, but ordinarily fails to reach, that goal. Like Shakespeare's dark comedies, Black Humor condemns man to a dying world; it never envisions, as do Shakespeare's early and late comedies, the possibilities of human escape from an aberrant environment into a forest milieu, as a ritual of the triumph of the green world over the waste land. Thus, at the conclusion of Bruce Jay Friedman's *Stern*, the protagonist is as alienated from "the kike man" and the suburban neighborhood he lives in as he was at the outset. Despite his efforts at *rapprochement*, he and society persist in the bonds of abnormality separating each other. The same comic divisiveness holds true for Benny Profane in Thomas Pynchon's *V.*, for Lester in Charles Wright's *The Wig*, for Oskar in Günter Grass's *The Tin Drum*, and for the narrator in Leonard Cohen's *Beautiful Losers*, to name a few of the many instances to be found in this fiction.

Black Humor's denial of social reconciliation or individual release is epitomized in the vision of Louis-Ferdinand Céline, who "worked the same beat" (Friedman admiringly acknowledges), "thought all your thoughts . . . was dumbfounded as many times a day as you are, long before you were born."[11] In *Journey to the End of the Night* the best that Bardamu can offer as a summation of his "aimless pilgrimage" through this "truly appalling, awful world" is that "life leaves you high and dry long before you're really through."[12] With numbness of heart, Bardamu acknowledges that neither person nor house can speak to him, that no one can find another in the darkness through which each is condemned to travel a long way by himself alone. Céline heralds the dead end of the eighteenth-century social and political ideal of the *philosophes*, memorably epitomized in William Godwin's boast that society is a collection of individuals.[13] And the many Black Humorists today who look on him as ur-progenitor continue to push farther into the Célinesque darkness—incredible as that seems—in determined exploration of the permutability of urban existence and the paralysis of human indifference.

8

The divisiveness of society is certainly one consequence of the individualizing bent of Protestant humanism of the past 500 years. But other causes peculiar to our century are equally discernible. One need only to contrast the Rome of Plautus and the London of Shakespeare to the New York of Friedman and the Los Angeles of Pynchon to see the change in social cohesion that has taken place. Whereas the Plautean Romans and the Shakespearean Londoners were members of cities whose districts added up to coherent and whole communities with identifiable classes and cultures, Friedman's New Yorkers and Pynchon's Angelenos live in cities no longer with centers, connected to each other by subways and freeways. Although they live elbow to elbow, they are separated by vast distances from the places of personal relationships: work, church, parental homes, recreation. Friedman's Everyman, Stern, daily faces a harrowing multi-houred trip to the office, among indifferent, or outright hostile, fellow commuters. Angelenos spend equal numbers of hours speeding down ribbons of concrete, each encased in his metal cocoon of an automobile, cut off from the intimate sounds and smells of human voices and bodies, permitted only the occasional blurred glimpse of a face through two panes of window glass as they whisk past one another. Benny Profane—Pynchon's man profaned—yo-yoing on the Times Square-Grand Central Station subway shuttle embodies the ultimate directionlessness of life in the modern city. In constant motion he lacks destination. Like Bardamu's restless movements from France to Africa to America back to France, life describes a pointless journey with death as the only true destination. It is this disjunctive world that moves the Black Humorist, in part, to arrest the traditional comic reconciliation of individual and society.

Black Humor differs also from current existentialist views of man in refusing to treat his isolation as an ethical situation. Friedman slyly ribs Stern's effort to offset his fearful solitariness. In the last scene of the novel, for example, Stern's self-conscious embrace of wife and child in the nursery becomes a parodic tableau of the holy family, mistimed and miscued:

> Now Stern walked around the room, touching the rugs to make sure they wouldn't fall on his son's face. Then he said, "I feel like doing some hugging," and knelt beside the sleeping

9

boy, inhaling his pajamas and putting his arm over him. His wife was at the door and Stern said, "I want you in here, too." She came over, and it occurred to him that he would like to try something a little theatrical, just kneel there quietly with his arms protectively draped around his wife and child. He tried it and wound up holding them a fraction longer than he'd intended. (p. 191)

Céline's dry tone and Parisian argot are similarly scornful of any mask other than the comic. With a matter-of-factness that suggests the laconic air of boredom (incongruously belied by the precipitous torrent of words), Bardamu recounts his indifference to life:

> Whatever people may care to make out, life leaves you high and dry long before you're really through.
> The things you used to set most store by, you one fine day decide to take less and less notice of, and it's an effort when you absolutely have to. You're sick of always hearing yourself talk. . . . You abbreviate. You renounce. Thirty years you've been at it, talking, talking . . . You don't mind now about being right. You lose even the desire to hang on to the little place you've reserved for yourself among the pleasures of life. . . . You're fed up. From now on, it's enough just to eat a little, to get a bit of warmth, and to sleep as much as you can on the road to nothing at all. . . . The only things that still mean anything very much to you are the little regrets, like never having found time to get round and see your old uncle at Bois-Colombes, whose little song died away forever one February evening. That's all one's retained of life, this little very horrible regret; the rest one has more or less successfully vomited up along the road, with a good many retchings and a great deal of unhappiness. One's come to be nothing but an aged lamppost of fitful memories at the corner of a street along which almost no one passes now. (pp. 459–460)

"If you're to be bored," Bardamu concludes, "the least wearisome way is to keep absolutely regular habits." Not suicide! that would be a nonsensical gesture of metaphysical despair or of archaic heroics. Todd Andrews reaches the same decision at the end of Barth's *The Floating Opera* when he recognizes that if there is no good reason why he should go on living, there is also no reason why he should die. This conception of its protagonist as the common man *manqué* is what makes Black Humor a somewhat limited vision capable of the specific aberrations of comedy, rather than the universal condition of tragedy.

We can gauge the degree of detachment practised by Black Humor if we compare these examples with the contrary moral renunciation of human kind that fires Schrella's decision at the conclusion of Heinrich Böll's *Billiards at Half-Past Nine*. A fugitive from Nazi Germany, Schrella has returned to his native city after an exile of more than twenty years. But he does not plan to stay. Unlike the rest of his countrymen and such Black Humor figures as Stern, he resolutely resists accommodation with the destructive powers of the past which persevere in the continuing forces of the present. As a continuing moral protest he persists in his rooming-house and hotel existence.

> "I'm afraid of houses you move into, then let yourself be convinced of the banal fact that life goes on and that you get used to anything in time. Ferdi would be only a memory, and my father only a dream. And yet they killed Ferdi, and his father vanished from here without a trace. They're not even remembered in the lists of any political organization, since they never belonged to any. They aren't even remembered in the Jewish memorial services, since they weren't Jewish . . . I can't live in this city because it isn't alien enough for me . . . my hotel room's exactly right. Once I shut the door behind me, this city becomes as foreign as all the others." (ch. 13)

Billiards at Half-Past Nine is black enough in its vision of man; but its fervid crusade to alter human nature, and its desperate rejection of society until such moral regeneration takes place, give it a tragic rather than comic mask. When he wishes, of course, Böll can write what passes for Black Humor. In *The Clown* he depicts the deterioration of Hans Schnier, a social misfit who cannot adjust to the hypocrisy of post-war Germany. Whereas Dostoevsky's Idiot spirals tragically heavenward, Böll's Clown winds down through Biedermeier instances of insult to a beggar's cushion in the Bonn train station. Like the irreverently treated heroes of *God Bless You, Mr. Rosewater* and *The Sot-Weed Factor*, Schnier the "wise fool" proves to be more foolish than wise. But even at this ebb tide of his life, Schnier unlike Schrella continues to seek out human company.

Like Böll's Clown the protagonist of Black Humor does not de-

11

spair with the savage bitterness of Nathanael West's Miss Lonely-hearts. Nor does he remain aloof, dismissing society with cold imperviousness, like Evelyn Waugh's Dennis Barlow. Rather, he worries about his place in it. Only after repeated rebuffs in his search for a relationship with others does he accept his empty existence with an angry shrug like Ferdinand Bardamu. He may be a booby like Friedman's Stern, a *naïf* like his Joseph, an anti-hero like Céline's Bardamu, a silly like Vonnegut's Eliot Rosewater, a pervert like Nabokov's Humbert Humbert, a clown like Heller's Yossarian, a fool like Barth's Ebenezer Cooke, a rogue like Berger's Jack Crabb, a drop-out like Grass's Oskar, a dupe like Pynchon's Herbert Stencil—but he is never an untouched innocent like Waugh's Paul Pennyfeather, nor a dismembered scapegoat like West's Lemuel Pitkin, nor an unwitting gull like Swift's Gulliver. At the end of *Decline and Fall* Paul Pennyfeather returns to college unchanged by his scarifying mishaps. At the end of *A Cool Million* Lemuel Pitkin is without thumb, leg, eye, teeth, scalp, indeed his very existence; yet is ironically a heroic witness to the American dream of success. The Black Humor protagonist is not, like these satiric foils, an authorial lens for analyzing the real, corrupt object of the satire. Nor does detachment mean for him withdrawal from the world, as it does for Gulliver, Candide, or Dennis Barlow. He is at once observer of, and participant in, the drama of dissidence, detached from and yet affected by what happens around him. Extremely conscious of his situation, he is radically different from the satiric puppets of Waugh and West, who bounce back like Krazy Kat from every cruel flattening as smooth and round as before, their minds unviolated by experience. His—and the author's—gaze is more often than not concentrated on what Conrad Knickerbocker has called the terrors and possibilities of the world we have brought into being in this century, and of the self-knowledge that this leads us toward.[14] His prison-house loneliness, forced upon him by existence, becomes a Célinesque journey to the end of the night.

The moral quality of society—the aim of satire—is not, according to Northrop Frye, the point of the comic resolution of an individual and a group.[15] Nor is it the objective of Black Humor, which resists any final accommodation. As Scholes notes, the Black Humorist is not concerned with what to do about life but with how

12

to take it.[16] This is not to say that he has no moral position, but only to suggest that this position is *implicit*. He may challenge the trances and hysterias of society, as Conrad Knickerbocker suggests,[17] but he does not ordinarily urge choice on us. He seeks rather a comic perspective on both tragic fact and moralistic certitude. In extreme instances, for example some of Kurt Vonnegut's writings, this attitude of mind will lead to the novel's refusal to take its implied moral position seriously. *The Sot-Weed Factor* has been faulted for its abdication of responsibility to answer the questions it raises about intrinsic values, and *Catch-22* for its central evasiveness as regards war, for its not having a point of view, an awareness of what things should or should not be.[18] Such is the ultimate ethical and aesthetic chaos that these novels risk in their rage for an inclusive purchase on reality.

The skepticism of the Black Humorist suggests an explanation for the distinctly metaphysical bent and American identity of this fiction. Can a writer convinced of the truth of a closed ethical, philosophical, or religious system conceptualize human experience in the terms of Black Humor? I think not. Undeviating acceptance of Christianity would surely make it impossible to produce an anti-God novel like Robert Coover's *The Universal Baseball Association, Inc.—J. Henry Waugh Prop.* other than as an unconvincing pastiche. It is his ardent Catholicism that prompts Heinrich Böll to castigate his bourgeois characters for giving their allegiance to the German economic miracle rather than to the Catholic religious values they nominally profess, and accounts for *The Clown*'s suffering from artistic and philosophical confusion and ultimately for not corresponding to the Black Humor novels considered here. Günter Grass also professes to be a Catholic. His social skepticism, however, qualifies his religious dogmatism. In *The Tin Drum* he contains the two perspectives of Catholicism and Black Humor, content with a simple balance of contraries, especially the dichotomies of guilt and innocence, tempter and tempted, the Christlike and the Satanical, the Dionysian (Oskar's fascination for Rasputin) and the Apollonian (Oskar's attraction to Goethe), without compulsion to reconcile them.[19] His concentration on the outward oriented world of objects—the tin drum, fizz powder, the smells of the women in Oskar's life, the cartridge case, the skat playing of

Oskar's parents, his grandmother's petticoats—contributes to this intellectual neutrality, since objects are basically inimical to ideas, or to the resolution of ideas.[20] Consequently Grass's novels observe the frame of reference of Black Humor despite his commitment to traditional beliefs.

The literary tradition of the German and English novels also militates against the inconclusive version of life presented in the Black Humor novel. The German *Bildungsroman*, or *Entwicklungsroman*, presupposes a set of social, as well as moral and ethical, values, a substantive goal toward which the protagonist progresses in preparation for his adult role in the community. *The Tin Drum* conforms to this genre but parodies its fixed principles in its conception of Oskar's being born with awareness, of his being as cognizant of his world at three as at thirty, and in its uncertainty (and plurality) of point of view.[21] The English novel of manners similarly assumes a collective relevance, established social classes and codes of conduct—a context within which narrative conflict is developed. The American novel, short on *Entwicklung* and manners, is more receptive to the inconclusive exploration of ontological and epistemological questions of being, growth, and knowledge. In this respect, the Black Humor novel continues the quest of the *Pequod*, its route updated and its procedure modernized.

It is not accidental probably that the two European writers, other than Grass and Céline, identified with Black Humor—Vladimir Nabokov and Jorge Luis Borges—exhibit a disillusioned cosmopolitanism acquired by the accidents of choice and of history that transcends the literary and cultural suppositions of their Russian and Argentinian heritages. To them has been "given bad times in which to live"[22] in greater measure than is man's normal lot; and their excruciating sense of the instability of life pervades the texture and substance of their fiction. "We are creatures of chance in an absolute void" (p. 324), "the *true* Present . . . an instant of zero duration" (p. 417), Nabokov has Van Veen exclaim in *Ada*, "—unless we be artists ourselves" (p. 324). Only in "the act of artistic correction" is "the pang of the Present" (p. 418) given durability. Heirs of this century's national tensions and philosophical uncertainties, their stories are parodies of man's mistaken faith historically and philosophically in cultural continuity and ideational permanence. Nor is it accidental that Kurt Vonnegut has waited longest of the Black Humorists for recognition. His novels are not organized according to one fictional kind but follow multiple modes, at once novel of manners, confessional journal, science fiction, social satire, detective story, soap opera, and slick magazine tale. The resultant farrago of literary syntaxes has bewildered and offended both British and American readers, whose expectations are never consistently satisfied. At any rate, Black Humor has remained, with the exception of the few European writers mentioned, a predominantly American phenomenon of the sixties, whose anxieties proceeding from pluralism, conformity, and an irresolute value system give it both its method and its subject.

NOTES TO CHAPTER I

1. Bruce Jay Friedman, Foreword to *Black Humor* (New York, 1965), pp. x–xi. The same essay with slight changes is reprinted as "Those Clowns of Conscience" in *Book Week* (July 15, 1965).

2. *Ibid.*, pp. vii–viii. I have quoted here from the version in *Book Week*.

3. *Ibid.*, p. xi.

4. *The Fabulators* (New York, 1967), pp. 35–46.

5. "Humor with a Mortal Sting," *New York Times Book Review*, LXIX, pt. 2 (September 27, 1964), 3, 60–61. Cf. Richard Schickel, "The Old Critics and the New Novel," *Wisconsin Studies in Contemporary Literature*, V (1964), 26–36.

6. Other attempts to deal with Black Humor include Richard Kostelanetz, "The Point Is That Life Doesn't Have Any Point," *New York Times Book Review*, LXX (June 6, 1965), 3, 28–30; reprinted as "The American Absurd Novel" in *The World of Black Humor*, ed. Douglas M. Davis (New York, 1967), pp. 306–313; Robert Buckeye, "The Anatomy of the Psychic Novel," *Critique*, IX (1967), 33–45; Charles D. Peavy, "Larry McMurtry and Black Humor: A Note on the Last Picture Show," *Western American Literature*, II (1967), 223–227; Douglas M. Davis, "Introduction," *The World of Black Humor* (New York, 1967); Koji Numasawa, "Black Humor: An American Aspect," *Studies in English Literature* (University of Tokyo), XLIV (1968), 177–193; Eugene McNamara, "The Absurd Style in Contemporary American Literature," *Humanities Association Bulletin* (Canada), XIX (1968), 44–49; Burton Feldman, "Anatomy of Black Humor," *Dissent* (March–April 1968); reprinted in *The American Novel Since World War II*, ed. Marcus Klein (New York, 1969), pp. 224–228; and Joseph J. Waldemeir, "Only an Oc-

casional Rutabaga: American Fiction Since 1945," *Modern Fiction Studies,* XV (1969–70), 467–481.

7. "Black Humor: Its Causes and Cure," *Colorado Quarterly,* XVII (1968), 57–64.

8. Josh Greenfield, "Bruce Jay Friedman Is Hanging by His Thumbs," *New York Times Magazine* (January 14, 1968).

9. Mark Spilka discusses these distinctions in *Dickens and Kafka: A Mutual Interpretation* (Bloomington, Ind., 1963), p. 262.

10. *English Institute Essays 1948* (New York, 1949), pp. 58–73; reprinted in *Theories of Comedy,* ed. Paul Lauter (New York, 1964), pp. 450–460, from which I quote.

11. *Black Humor,* p. viii.

12. (New York: New Directions Paperback, 1960), pp. 504 and 459. All subsequent references are to this edition.

13. *An Enquiry Concerning Political Justice,* bk. II, ch. 2.

14. "Humor with a Mortal Sting," *New York Times Book Review,* LXIX, pt. 2 (September 27, 1964), p. 61.

15. "The Argument of Comedy," *Theories of Comedy,* p. 453.

16. *The Fabulators,* p. 43.

17. "Humor with a Mortal Sting," p. 61.

18. Cf. Robert Garis, "What Happened to John Barth?" *Commentary,* LXXXV (October, 1966), 80–82; and Earl Rovit, "The Novel as Parody: John Barth," *Critique* VI (1963), 77–85; John M. Muste, "Better to Die Laughing: The War Novels of Joseph Heller and John Ashmead," *Critique,* V (1962), 16–27; and John Wain, "A New Novel about Old Troubles," *Critical Quarterly,* V (1963), 168–173.

19. Cf. Leslie A. Willson, "The Grotesque Everyman in Günter Grass's *Die Blechtrommel,*" *Monatshefte,* LVIII (1966), 131–138.

20. Cf. W. G. Cunliffe, "Aspects of the Absurd in Günter Grass," *Wisconsin Studies in Contemporary Literature,* VII (1966), 311–327.

21. Cf. Cunliffe, *ibid.*; and Robert Maurer, "The End of Innocence: Günter Grass's *The Tin Drum,*" *Bucknell Review,* XVI (1968), 45–65.

22. From Borges's tribute to his Argentine forbear Juan Crisóstomo Lafinur, in the Prologue to "A New Refutation of Time."

II

THE METAPHYSICS OF MULTIPLICITY; AND, THE THOUSAND AND ONE MASKS OF JOHN BARTH

I

To the satirist there are false versions of reality and true versions. Whispering Glades in Waugh's *The Loved One* is a false ordering of reality, the traditionalism identified with English country houses a true ordering. The illogicality of action rampant in the Horatio Alger world of West's *A Cool Million* does not ultimately deny an underlying faith in the Puritan ethic of industry and perseverence. To the Black Humorist, contrariwise, all versions of reality are mental constructs. He agrees with Todd Andrews's reflection at the end of *The Floating Opera* that "Nothing has intrinsic value" (ch. 26). No principle is aprioristically truer than another. Falsity obtains only when we mistakenly assume that one verbal construct morally or intellectually pre-empts all others.

The Black Humorist sees life as a maze that is mutiple and endless rather than unitive and conclusive. The human dilemma posed by such a view is given full voice in Barth's *The Sot-Weed Factor*. "*Ah, God,*" Ebenezer Cooke writes to his sister,

> *it were an easy Matter to choose a Calling, had one all Time to live in! I should be fifty Years a Barrister, fifty a Physician, fifty a Clergyman, fifty a Soldier! Aye, and fifty a Thief, and fifty a Judge! All Roads are fine Roads, beloved Sister, none more than another, so that with one Life to spend I am a Man*

17

barebumm'd at Taylors with Cash for but one pair of Breeches,
or a Scholar at Bookstalls with Money for a single Book; to
choose ten were no Trouble; to choose one, impossible! All
Trades, all Crafts, all Professions are wondrous, but none is
finer than the rest together. I cannot choose, sweet Anna: twixt
Stools my Breech falleth to the Ground! (ch. 2)

Rather than acquiesce like Ebenezer into immobility before the
multiplicity of choice, the Black Humorist prefers like Burlingame
to confront as many combinations of this kaleidoscope of shapes,
actions, and possibilities as he can. And like Burlingame he culti-
vates an indiscriminative appetite, along with a detached attitude,
equally receptive to the bizarre and the mundane, the startling and
the familiar. *Lolita* documents without editorial indignation the
drab and furtive bowers of Hymen that masquerade as the proud
American institution, the Motel. *The Sot-Weed Factor* luxuriates in
the venery and political venality of the colonial American. *A*
Mother's Kisses links the prurient glimpses of sex by a seventeen-
year-old to the boyish collecting of baseball cards; it defines the
sacrosanct fellowship of father and son as a tension of day-long
silence broken only by such intimacies as "I buy a paper here," "I
usually stand at this end [of the subway] and hold on to a strap,"
and "I only take a fast bite" for lunch (pp. 14–15). *V.* soberly tells
us about wild disoriented hunts through the sewers of New York
for alligators grown from pet reptiles flushed down the toilet or
escaped down street drains. *The Tin Drum* limns the pleasures of
fizz powder. The popular forms of detective story, science fiction,
and western offer as many attractions as traditionally serious literary
vehicles. Quantitative, not qualitative, comprehension then is the
Black Humorist's strategy, with the hope that out of this wide-
angled vision, as out of a programmed computor, will issue verbal
patterns meaningful to our experience.

Both Friedman and Knickerbocker have argued, as an apolo-
getics for the distortion of experience in Black Humor, that "traditional forms cannot accommodate a reality which now includes a
Jack Ruby."[1] Unquestionably Black Humor reflects in its fictional
materials the metaphysics of its vision. This metaphysics, like Mc-
Luhan's cool world of electronic viewing, posits a discontinuous
and instantaneous universe, where action and consequence are mon-

strously disparate, and where hierarchical order has disappeared. Hence writers of Black Humor have had to devise fictional forms that are enormously self-conscious, aware not only of their position but of the endless other possible orbits that stand in relation to them. Their aim, to use the words of Richard Kostelanetz in reference to Thomas Pynchon,[2] is to formulate symbols for a metaphysical reality that suggests not ambiguity but unbounded multiplicity.

The difficulties in realizing such a program are awesome. The immediate dangers are disunity and inconclusiveness. In devising solutions of these inherent problems, Borges has been among the most daringly inventive, as well as the most willing to face the implications for his art of his cosmological vision. The brevity of his *ficciones*—some as short as three, four, or five pages—represents an effort to place boundaries on the elusive matter and endless indirection of his cosmologies. His formulation of stories that masquerade as essays, complete with all the scholarly paraphernalia of footnotes, bibliographical information, and advancing of evidence, is another way not only of blurring the distinction between the historical and the imaginative but also of fixing the permutations of his world-pictures within the confines of critiques. *The Book of Imaginary Beings* offers a more radical artistic equivalent to the inclusive vision of Black Humor. At once a dictionary, a modern bestiary, a handbook of antiquarian lore, a commonplace book of favorite monsters, and an exercise in literary and linguistic rehabilitation, the work (with index!) consists of separate entries, compilations or individual essay-stories drawn from disparate sources on each fabulous animal. Conceived as a book in which "the possibilities of permutation border on the infinite," the authors (Borges collaborated with Margaritta Guerro) cheerfully acknowledge in the Preface to the 1957 first edition in Spanish that they do "not exhaust the sum total of imaginary animals." In subsequent editions (1967 in Spanish and 1969 in English) they have both compiled additional articles and "altered a good number of the original articles, correcting, adding, or revising material" (Preface to the 1969 English-language edition). The latter was further "Revised, Enlarged and Translated by Norman Thomas di Giovanni in collaboration with the author" (so announced on the title page), introducing an additional note of indeterminacy. One does not know what has been written by Borges, what by Margaritta Guerro, and what interpolated by di Giovanni. As noted in the Preface to the 1967 edition, "A book of this kind is unavoidably incomplete; each new edition forms the basis of future editions, which themselves grow on endlessly." Indeed, the potentially all-embracing nature of the book is ironically remarked by the authors:

> The title of this book would justify the inclusion of Prince Hamlet, of the point, of the line, of the surface, of n-dimensional hyperplanes and hypervolumes, of all generic terms, and perhaps of each one of us and of the godhead. In brief, the sum of all things—the universe. We have limited ourselves, however, to what is immediately suggested by the words "imaginary beings"; we have compiled a handbook of the strange creatures conceived through time and space by the human imagination. (Preface to the 1967 edition)

In the organization of such disparate materials into aesthetic wholes, however, literary inventiveness has tended to lag behind the visual arts in the past several decades. The constructions of H. C. Westermann, and the Los Angeles assemblage artists Kienholz, Conner, and Von Huene are instances of the skill with which the anarchic possible has been disciplined into unified statements. Stephan Von Huene's animated figures, especially, inventively explore the endless mutations inherent in a world of multiplicity. The most expressive of this world view are those pieces which combine the mechanisms of the player piano and the animation of mechanical toys. His *Kaleidoscopic Dog* consists of cymbals, percussion devices and claves mounted over a wood box containing a pneumatic drive mechanism, on top of which is installed an animated leather-covered wood sculpture of a dog. As the music plays, the dog moves its legs, head, and mouth as if physically responsible for the music, an animation patently belied by its structure and by the obvious player-piano music-roll programming. Five perforated rolls in continuous loops repeat their information endlessly. Of different lengths, the relation between the rolls is constantly changing. Hence the resultant music never repeats itself. Von Huene's *Washboard Band* produces a similar ironic commentary on the heterogeneity and inconclusiveness of this world. Its vertical arrangement of a washboard and two slender boxes suggests the human figure, as Hall Glicksman notes in a pamphlet on four of the artist's works shown at the Los Angeles County Art Museum in 1969, "reinforced as the beaters strumming the washboard begin to move like fingers and hands." In these animated fantasies, the distinctions between human, animal, and mechanical blur. The machines convey the hallucination of performing music which they have composed themselves, music whose endless mutations seem to derive from the infinite variables of the universe. Insistently rendering a sense of controlled confinement to each piece, as a counter action to the amorphous stream of sound, are the mechanical rendering of the information and the rigid frames of the sculpture.

The serial sculptures of Donald Judd represent a contrary reductive (or minimalist) statement about the plurality of our world. In his stainless steel boxes suspended one above the other in serial extension from a wall, Judd offers contrary to one's expectations not sameness but endless variation and deception. Their straight-on semblance of solidity is disclosed, when the viewer shortens his distance from them, to be hollow boxes with transparent plexiglass tops and bottoms through which one glimpses sides and angles of the boxes above and below. Each change in one's focal distance *vis à vis* the boxes alters their ambience. Such sculpture (and Judd as well as others have done many versions of it) contains *in potentia* an inexhaustible number of different relationships and perspectives.

In the past decade much energy of the Black Humorists has gone into devising narrative strategies that would similarly weaken the restrictive implications of the limited and incomplete sensibility governing conventional handling of narration and of point of view.

At least six kinds of deployment are used to suggest the self-conscious awareness that the world of our sensibility impinges upon, and is invaded in turn by, the worlds of other sensibilities. (1) The careful Jamesian distinction between narrator and author is blurred, allowing for the introduction of authorial responses to the narrator's vision not verified by the experience of the narrative. Both Céline and Nabokov adopt this maneuver in the conclusions of *Journey to the End of the Night* and *Lolita*. A startling variation is the homogenizing, as Barth terms it,[3] of first and third person, in some of Donleavy's and Nabokov's work, and in Vonnegut's latest novel *Slaughterhouse-Five*. (2) Corollary to the narratorial blur is the felt presence of the author throughout the novel. Nabokov employs this tactic in *Lolita* with the skill of a master chess player. He plants clues, introduces his own signature of the passionate pursuit of lepidoptery, arbitrarily alters Humbert's physical appearance—all as a reminder to the reader that the omniscient control of the author is never in doubt. Like Nabokov, Borges never for long remains passively removed from the manipulative boundaries of his story. Both men delight in the erudite reference and the bibliographical note, as often as not falsely concocted to mislead the reader. (3) The human sense of time and the distinctions of history are redefined, until the present becomes a parodic reconstruction of the past, a compendium of all the human exercises in abstraction designed to impose connectiveness on the intervals of time. Barth, Borges, Coover, Nabokov, and Pynchon are all inventive practitioners of this ardent "betrayal" of experience. (4) Literary parody offers these writers another dimension of self-consciousness, for disclosing how our verbal constructs are subjective perceptions of reality. Their parodies—and almost all use this device with increasing frequency—comically remind us that other worlds, other patterns of reality, exist concurrently with the ones of our making. Their multidimensional presentations of human experience correct our tragic tendency (one thinks of Humbert Humbert's error) to mistake the mirror of one's mind as a true record of the *Ding an sich*. Epistemologically they represent efforts, in the phrase of Alfred Appel, "to exhaust the 'fictional gestures' " which would reduce the ineffable qualities of human experience to a convention of language.[4] (5) The revered Aristotelian dogma of plot, while not read out of the canon, is obscured by a broadening of the independent role of incidents and surface details. In short, although the plot obviously develops the theme, it does not encompass the whole of the thematic statement that the novel makes. Hence, plot and theme are not always in focus, permitting apparently irrelevant incidents to develop bi-focally in concurrence with the plot a related but more inconclusive vision of life. Friedman, along with Céline, Heller, and Vonnegut, generally employ this tactic in their novels. In *Stern*, for example, the symbolic action of the narrative fails to give us the full statement of theme. Whereas the plot deals with a Jewish protagonist's effort to avenge an insult to his wife, the novel is thematically much more ambitious than the subject of anti-Semitism;

22

it casts a much wider net not only in its references to Stern's fantasies of sexual and social violence but also in its references to the larger social arena in which these random acts purportedly occur. (6) Activities and thoughts appear in their negative aspects, expanding our sensibilities, like Alice through the Looking Glass, with the hint of new amazements. Thus is suggested to our consciousness the suspicion that the arrangement of experience into either/or equations falsifies by delimitation the alternative infinites of *and* and *and*. Grass for instance organizes much of *The Tin Drum* according to this principle, as also does Vonnegut in his novels.

II

In the self-conscious re-orientation of experience found in the Black Humor novel—in its desperate desire to unwind the skein of experience to the bare spool—we have what Barth (in reference specifically to Jorge Luis Borges) has called contemporary literature's baroque exhaustion of the frightening guises of reality.[5] This *regressus in infinitum* is a logical outgrowth of the world posited in Black Humor writing. As one of its anthologists has remarked, "There are no certainties in Black Humor,"[6] as there are none in the world it chronicles. The warrant officer sick with malaria in *Catch-22* voices the central vision of Black Humor when he remarks to Yossarian that

> "There just doesn't seem to be any logic to this system of rewards and punishment. Look what happened to me. If I had gotten syphilis or a dose of clap for my five minutes of passion on the beach instead of this damned mosquito bite, I could see some justice. But malaria? *Malaria*? Who can explain malaria as a consequence of fornication? . . . Just for once I'd like to see all these things sort of straightened out, with each person getting exactly what he deserves. It might give me some confidence in this universe." (ch. 17)

Not just the warrant officer's words but also the setting for his statement, the base hospital, provide Black Humor with what is practically a literary convention. Borges' vision of human experience as a labyrinth is a near perfect metaphysical conceit for Black Humor's world picture. Another almost equally appropriate is un-

23

diagnosed illness. One thinks of Yossarian's puzzling liver condition, Eliot Rosewater's amnesia, Sebastian Dangerfield's debilitating malaises, Cabot Wright's blackouts, Jacob Horner's and Ebenezer Cooke's recurrent immobilities, Oskar's madness, Funes' vertiginous exhaustion, Humbert Humbert's nervous breakdowns, Stern's ulcer, Joseph's father's mysterious back ailment, Meg's periodic sieges of sitting around in a bath robe. Friedman's novels, particularly, abound in enigmatic balloonings of arm and head, in inexplicable lapses and convalescences. While recovering from an attack of swelling, Joseph expresses surprise that anything sick ever heals. "One day, he felt, it would be announced that the whole germ theory of disease was a hoax, that there was no such thing as a germ . . . that all medicines were silly, doctors could learn all they needed to know in two weeks of school and that when people got better it was a wild coincidence" (*A Mother's Kisses*, p. 126). Implicit in Joseph's expectations is a denial of the meaningful relatedness of actions, on which the accepted empirical notions of the physical world are posited. If causal sequence (*non sequitur*) and temporal sequence (*post hoc*; *ergo, propter hoc*) are questioned, then technically all history may be a sham—as Black Humorists have been pointing out delightedly at great length. Without a logic of events to narrow the possibilities of an action to one or several consequences, a Pandora's box of possibilities is uncapped. Thus, at a signal from the leader of an overcoated gang after he had distributed bars of halvah, a girl may undress "as though she always disrobed after halvah servings" (*A Mother's Kisses*, p. 186). If her nudity follows such illogical directives, why could it not just as easily be triggered by an afternoon on the ski slopes, or a snappy speech by the Vice-President, or an hour of TV cartoons?

In a world containing inexhaustible possibilities of action, not only will the terror of daily life with its mandatory decisions axiomatically wax out of all proportion to the situation, but repetition and transformation will become commonplace. The assemblage of the familiar is inevitable when the maze of experience is *au fond* directionless and goalless. It offers one means of shoring up the known against the unknown. At the same time, the interminable duplication of things figures as the equivalent of reality. In this light the structural peculiarities of some well-known Black Humor novels, which have attracted critical attention on that account, become explicable: the compulsive return again and again to the same action in *Catch-22*; the inexhaustible guises and disguises in *The Sot-Weed Factor*, the transformations of places and persons, with the same initial letter in *V.*; and the endless refractions of mirror words and images, puns, parodies, and doubles in *Lolita*.

Even more to the point is the shift from refined selectivity to omnibus appetite for experience in so many of these novels. Innocence, or ignorance as Burlingame castigates it, becomes "the true Original Sin our souls are born in," "whereof the Knowledged must bear the burthen." "Not that Adam *learned*, but that he had to learn" (*The Sot-Weed Factor*, III, 21)—that is the reality that Ebenezer and all Adam's sons, *ipsit* Black Humor, must contend with. "Through being thrown out of every place," Bardamu consoles himself, "you'll surely finish up by finding out what it is that frightens all those bloody people so" (pp. 218–219). Hence his tireless journeying to face the terror of war, the horror of colonial Africa, the hysteria of industrial America, and the nausea of the slums of Paris. This quest collapses together centuries of events in Barth and Pynchon's novels, and links earth with intergalactic space in Vonnegut's novels. In both *The Sirens of Titan* and *Cat's Cradle* the joke on man is that he may comb through all the debris of this world and still not learn towards what end his life has moved, since the purposefulness of terrestrial actions may be tied to extra-human cosmic ends. What preoccupies these authors is not desire for experience itself so much as a need to find, in Ebenezer Cooke's words, an Ariadne's thread marking our "path through the labyrinth of Life" (II, 3)—a need to cajole out of experience all its variations, as a way of getting at the causes of reality, of connecting us with our starting place. Like Menelaus on the shores of Pharos in Euripedes' play, exhorting direction from the Proteus of life,[7] they are less bent on judging the multiple appearances of reality than on simply knowing them, as the only desperate way left to wring from experience a modicum of sanity, perhaps of salvation. Is not the vitriolic name-calling engaged in by two prostitutes in the kitchen at Malden (*The Sot-Weed Factor*, II, 31), in which two languages, French and English, are exhausted of their stock of epithets just such an exuberant exercise in containment of a small sphere of human activity?

Contrariwise, is not the body ethic of the hippy commune an extreme solution of this dilemma? Celebrated in the rock musical *Hair*, it substitutes a sensationist philosophy for a suspect value system, and a life style of multiplicity for one of moral selectivity. Any ethic based on such a philosophy though has its own limitations. The human sensibility is neither inexhaustible nor macrotabular. Yet it is called upon to react pluralistically and endlessly, since every renewal of sense of community, of relatedness, must be physically realized. Similarly, it is expected to embrace every variety of experience while retaining the ability to discriminate among them the fake from the authentic. Hence there may be a philosophical rationale of sorts to buttress the socio-economic rejection of ownership, or (in Blakean terms) of binding another to one's delight, as explanation of the sexual promiscuity of these "families"; but there is still the difficulty of maintaining the ethic against an expense of energy and a waste of indiscrimination.

One of the virtues of Leonard Cohen's *Beautiful Losers* is the honesty with which it depicts the inevitable bankruptcy of a body ethic. In a serious exploration of the possibilities of realizing the full potential of man, in the creation of the New Man not restricted to "genital imperialism" but erotogenic in "All parts of the body" (ch. 12), the novel opposes the value system of a body ethic (embodied in F. and his mistress the Indian girl Edith) to that of a soul ethic (represented by the seventeenth-century Mohawk Indian saint Catherine Tekakwitha). The correspondences between the two women in physical appearance, ethnic backgrounds, and in narrative circumstances are extensive, pointing up the ultimate bankruptcy of both value systems. If Edith in her search for union with the New Man (F.) of total erotogeny commits suicide as the aftermath of her sexual flagellation of flesh, Catherine in her yearning for union with the Christ God of the soul also dies suicidally in penitential flagellation of her flesh. The losers, as Cohen sees it, are all those—both worshippers of the body and witnesses of the soul— who put their faith in a value system: not only F. burnt out syphilitically, Edith exhausted sexually, and Catherine flayed mercilessly on her bed of pain; but also Larry, the narrator and betrayed husband of Edith, who fails each test devised by F. to transform him into another New Man and who ends totally alone in a frozen tree house, alienated from his countrymen and bereft of the two people he loved; and also by inference all Canadians caught by the exigencies of birth in the frightening vacuum of a country historically anonymous and geographically anomalous.[8]

Beautiful Losers extrapolates (as Robert Boyers shows) from Norman O. Brown's "theories of the adult body as fundamentally erotogenic" and "as the proper medium for mystical experience,"[9] a radical formula for the confrontation of chaos. It is to his credit that Cohen, a popular troubador for the generation which has espoused a body ethic, does not succumb to the temptation to falsify or to sentimentalize the inadequacies of the new religion but depicts in exhaustive detail the superhuman effort required to realize such an ideal and the inexorable failure given the limited capacity of man.

Unlike Cohen's desperate gamble to reach some kind of détente with life, most Black Humorists are content with more limited gains. The exchange between the two prostitutes in *The Sot-Weed Factor* is aesthetically manageable, as are Eben and Burlingame's Hudibrastic rhyming contest and Barth's parody of the eighteenth-century novel and world picture. Still, even in the firmly defined expositions of reality that comprise *The Sot-Weed Factor*, *V.*, *Lolita*, *Little Big Man*, and *The Tin Drum*, the stretch of these writers for an omnibus purchase on experience taxes their ingenuity to find ways of encompassing their material, of giving outline to it. The ideal situation, given a metaphysics of multiplicity, would be the "multiform, instantaneous and almost intolerably precise world" (p. 65) of Ireneo Funes in Borges's story "Funes the Memorious." Capable of total perception and infallible memory, he could reconstruct every whole day in his life, each reconstruction naturally requiring another whole day. Unfortunately, in the "heat and pressure of a reality as indefatigable as that which day and night converged upon the hapless Ireneo," there were only details, a teeming world of implacable memory resistant to thought, for as Borges asserts, "To think is to forget differences, generalize, make abstractions" (p. 66). Indeed, logic, comparison, contrast, the range of thought which depends on some kind of relationship is antithetical to a pluralistic world.

The conclusions are inexorable. If we live in a world without visible cause and effect, where even comprehensive little packets of time and space no longer comfortably orient us, we remain undefined experientially. We exist in unrelatedness, like the inhabitants of Heaven in Eliot Rosewater's unfinished novel, who lament that

> There is no inside here. There is no outside here. To pass through the gates in either direction is to go from nowhere to nowhere and from everywhere to everywhere. (*God Bless You, Mr. Rosewater*, ch. 7)

Restriction then not in the ordinary sense but in its contrary guise of boundarylessness poses for these writers a major problem. How to cope with endless multiplicity? How to order and orient experience, without denying its inherent disorientation? This central question clearly affects the aesthetic strategies of Black Humor.

It is understandable why plot and structure loom more importantly than characterization in much Black Humor; why the patterns of history-philosophy-myth and the arrangements of society supply these novels so frequently with their forms; and why the ironic parody of these orderings affords their authors a favored method of conveying the coherencies of civilization and at the same time chaos of random alternatives.

In a limited sense, then, Robert Scholes is right in noting the interest of the Black Humorists with construction; but he minimizes their seriousness when he characterizes this concern as playful or artful. Like the Painterly and Post-Painterly movements, the Black Humorist's intensive search through form for the springs of twentieth-century existence is worthy of our attention. If he cannot be numbered among those moral activists who change the visible face of things, he is nevertheless, in his passionate concentration on the hallucinations of reality, as Knickerbocker insists, one of the "keepers of conscience."[10] Among the writers of contemporary fiction, the Black Humorist is conspicuously risking the resources of the imagination to instruct us anew in ways of perceiving reality.

III

The logic of pluralism demands that its practitioners make ever new starts, venture beyond ever "New thresholds, new anatomies!"[11] Among contemporary novelists, none has sought more strenuously and more consciously to create an omnibus "literature of exhausted possibility,"[12] aside from Borges, than Barth (in this country), Günter Grass (in Europe), and Nabokov (in Estotiland-Terra-Antiterra). All three have relied heavily on the paraphernalia of doubles, disguises, and mirrored refractions in their probings of whether reality consists ultimately of the one or the many, of unity or multiplicity. One thinks of Ebenezer and his twin sister, Burlingame and his half brothers, Humbert and his alter ego Quilty, Oskar the three year old and Oskar the thirty year old; or of Lolita forced to choose (in Humbert's jocular words) "between a Hamburger and a Humburger" (II, 3). These are ambulatory skylarks into the Daedalian maze in *jeu d'esprit* anticipations of worlds glimpsed from afar and soon to be explored. In comparison to *The Sot-Weed Factor*, *The Tin Drum*, and *Lolita*, the later plunges into the "weary labyrinth"[13] are belabored efforts at historical-mythical-allegorical fabling. *Giles Goat-Boy*, *Dog Years*, and *Ada* are encyclopedic histories of their authors's worlds, reinventions pursued relentlessly to the final exhaustive pun and ultimate self-fulfilling parody. To move from the belly of WESCAC to the pit of the Brauxel potash mine to the lumber room of Ardis Hall is to wander through the labyrinthine galleries of western civilization. The achievements here are endgames. Like Joyce's *Finegans Wake*, they present us with forms exhausted, possibilities fully realized. In this respect, the methods of Black Humor ironically have displayed a predilection for early obsolescence, forcing the Black Humorist to be continuously inventive, a magician surprising us with a new animal each time he reaches into his hat.

The gesture of perennial renewal demanded of Black Humor is not undertaken lightly. To date Barth has been one of its most seriously self-immolative fabulist adventurers. He did not embrace the role of Menelaus on the beach at Pharos wrestling with Proteus for his literary identity with the alacrity of George Goat-Boy determined to make himself a culture hero. The facts would indicate that he stumbled somewhat onto this novelistic path when he broke free of the "Maryland-based verisimilitude"[14] of *The Floating Opera* and *The End of the Road* into the historical amplitudes of *The Sot-Weed Factor*. Barth has admitted to being ignorant of the patterns of mythic heroism at the time of his writing *The Sot-Weed Factor*.[15]

Nevertheless, Ebenezer and Burlingame in combination exhibit most of the characteristics of the culture hero listed by Lord Raglan in *The Hero*. Once he learned of the hero with a thousand faces, as mapped by such comparative mythographers as Lord Raglan and Joseph Campbell, he recognized the usefulness of the archetype in his exploration of the disease of modern life—Todd Andrews's, Jake Horner's, and Ebenezer Cooke's malaise, *cosmopsis* Jake Horner tags it—the uncertainty of an essential "I."

The British existential psychiatrist R. D. Laing has defined this inability of man to experience himself as real, as "a *basic existential position of . . . ontological insecurity*." In the normal physical and psychological growth process Laing writes, the individual experiences himself as an entity, "real, alive, whole,"

> as differentiated from the rest of the world in ordinary circumstances so clearly that his identity and autonomy are never in question; as a continuum in time; as having an inner consistency, substantiality, genuineness, and worth; as spatially co-extensive with the body; and, usually, as having begun in or around birth and liable to extinction with death.

By these means, man achieves "a firm core of ontological security."[16] More than one commentator on the midtwentieth century has bleakly contended that the plight of our society is its abnormal ontological insecurity. According to Erich Fromm, "everything, including ourselves, is being abstractified." "It is the fact that *man does not experience himself as the active bearer of his own powers and richness, but as an impoverished 'thing,' dependent on powers outside of himself, unto whom he has projected his living substance*."[17] The pervasive preoccupation with the problem of self is reflected in the titles of many recent books: Wylie Sypher's *Loss of the Self in Modern Literature and Art* (1962), Lionel Trilling's *The Opposing Self* (1955), R. D. Laing's *The Divided Self* (1960) and *Self and Others* (1969), Rollo May's *Man's Search for Himself* (1953), Paul Tillich's *The Courage to Be* (1952), Allen Wheelis's *The Quest for Identity* (1958), and Erich Fromm's *Man for Himself* (1947) and *The Sane Society* (1955).

Intent on testing whether the current loss of self is simply the latest multiagonist masking a mythic identity, Barth deliberately employs the hero with a thousand faces for his protagonist in *Giles*

Goat-Boy. In this act, Barth indicates, if the early novels had not already made it clear, that the Great Labyrinth is imaged for him less by the cosmos than by the mind, less by the incoherent social scene than by the disintegrated self. His literary aim then is not, like that of Borges and the younger Black Humorists dealt with in Chapter 4, to create a paradigmatic design more coherent than that found in the world. Rather, Barth's preoccupation is with isolating and identifying the ineluctable sense of what it is to be human. He fails in *Giles Goat-Boy* essentially because the mythic prototype he parodies is too hybrid a form, too diffusely "hit-and-miss" a system.[18] Gerhard Joseph is right to conclude that Barth, "in his depletion of the picaresque mode, in his erudite catalogues of ideas, or in his name-calling contest between the prostitutes," was trying in *The Sot-Weed Factor* "to convey the impression that sheer exhaustiveness for its own sake contributes to a meaningful comic [cosmic?] order."[19] The literary form of *The Sot-Weed Factor*, its correspondences to the novels of Fielding and Richardson limited its boundaries, as did also Barth's divided attention to the human and the cosmic labyrinths. In *Giles Goat-Boy* Barth was unhampered by such generic considerations and went all out to compress within the covers of one book the whole story of man, "from primitive animal to autonomous computer."[20] That the effort did not lead Barth to a redefinition of man meaningful for our time but left him like George Goat-Boy, with all the old categories, contradictions, and appearances still as ill-defined and as imminent of the primordial threat of chaos as ever, does not mean that the novel was altogether a dead end for Barth. With it he learned, as Borges seems to have known intuitively from the outset, that the objectivity of the mythographer, with his empirical arrangement of diverse materials, does not lead one to the heart of the matter, to the identification of the self, but merely to the accumulation of the flotsam and jetsam of civilization, the hero remaining the sum of his disparate parts, the quotient of his thousand and one faces. Barth also learned that if George was merely equivalent to the refractions of his thousand images, Oedipus offered a mythic correlative to the private self as well as scoring highest on "Lord Raglan's twenty-five prerequisites for ritual heroes."[21]

The "modern translation" of *The Tragedy of Taliped Decanus,*

31

a middle-American tragedy of "making it," with slangy diction and academic setting, is one of the more successful pieces of writing in *Giles Goat-Boy* (I, iii, 4). In this version of the Oedipus story, the problem of knowledge—here Oedipus's self-knowledge—is twisted out of its ethical frame of reference (as witnessed by the pun on "proph-prof") into a profane exposition of the "old Adam" in man. Taliped is less obsessed with the mystery of his aristocratic identity than with the knowledge that keeps winding him back to himself as sexual beast. Not the idea that he "murdered Pa" but that he "mounted Ma" monopolizes his horrified imagination. The perennial fascination of the nymphomaniac mother comes with a shock of recognition that the engineered consummation of Ebenezer's marriage to Joan Toast seems not to have stirred. The two-backed animal act of George and Anastasia in the Belly of WESCAC, however, confirms this iconoclastic vision of man. It is Joan Toast's and Anastasia's secret knowledge as females that "saves" both Ebenezer and George, leading them to the recovery of Malden and the salvation of the College, in short to the sexual urge to love and the existential urge to be, fundamental to all value systems.

The aftermath of *Giles Goat-Boy* has seen Barth return to personal origins, to his restatements of the Oedipal theme and to his inchoate urgings of self into artistic form, at which he had made a start in "Ambrose His Mark" and "Water-Message," published in 1963 prior to his writing of *Giles Goat-Boy*, and afterward resumed in "Autobiography" published in January 1968. These stories tentatively but insistently connect the mystery of one's sexual being (the preoccupations of Oedipus) with the authorial pains of fictional parturition. Especially compelling in "Water-Message" is the nine-year-old Ambrose's innocent conjuration of a grove of honey locusts into a jungle "labyrinth of intersecting footpaths" and "voluptuous fetidity." Here the boys have built a hideaway den, where one day they intrude upon the lovemaking of a sailor and his girl. The situation remains inexplicably exciting to the sexually uninitiated Ambrose, as also its objective correlative, the sheet of paper on which is penned "To whom it may concern" and "Yours truly," all between remaining blank, which washes ashore in a bottle and is picked up by Ambrose following the "flushing" of the lovers. Both the still-to-be-completed message and the interrupted lovers are harbingers of Ambrose's future, as worked out in the subsequent stories.

In "Title" and "Life-Story," published after *Giles Goat-Boy*, Barth fuses these dual modes of discovery of self into stories that are paradigms of the creative process, the fictional characters realized only to the extent that their storyteller can self-consciously imagine himself as a distinct person. But the possibilities of such *regressus in infinitum* are drastically limited. In "Life-Story," a desperate tongue-in-cheek echo of Borges's story "The Circular Ruins," Barth concludes, "and caused the 'hero' of his story to conclude,"

> that one or more of three things must be true: 1) his author was his sole and indefatigable reader; 2) he was in a sense his own author, telling his story to himself, in which case; and/or 3) his reader was not only tireless and shameless but sadistic, masochistic if he was himself.

This bleak cul-de-sac is prefaced by an authorial outburst at "You reader! You, dogged, uninsultable, print-oriented bastard," in language that alludes simultaneously and paradigmatically to McLuhan's dismissal of the Gutenberg sensibility, to Baudelaire's profane search through *Les Fleurs du Mal* for his identity,[22] and to Barth's compulsive fictional refractions of personality as a means of getting at human essence.

Neither "Title" nor "Life-Story" climaxes into a fully realized story. Process remains ever in an unfinished—and hence ultimately unknowable—state of becoming. In "Lost in the Funhouse" Barth returns to the seemingly more fruitful possibilities of Ambrose's rites-of-passage.

The funhouse—like Borges's garden of forking paths, or library of Babel, or lottery in Babylon—is a metaphor for the labyrinths of existence. Unlike Borges, whose perfect designs are intended as analogues of defective mythic and metaphysical systems of cosmic order,[23] Barth seizes on the mirror room of the funhouse, and on Ambrose's "coming of age" there, as a rendering of modern man's (and the contemporary novelist's) search through the distortions and "endless replication of his image in the mirrors" for ontological confirmation of his existence. "For whom is the funhouse fun?" the narrator asks. "Perhaps for lovers," he conjectures, and then adds: "For Ambrose it is *a place of fear and confusion*." Whereas Borges never asks from his "vertiginous symmetries" any knowledge beyond the aesthetic astonishment they engender, Barth assumes a persona who wants to find in the form of his story a sign of sorts of his ontological security. Pervasive to Borges's vision is his cheerful acceptance that he is nobody, dreamt by a God who is in turn the dream of another. He is "Borges," a creation of a "falsifying and magnifying" writer ("Borges and I"), like Shakespeare "Many and no one." Thus, Borges fancies Shakespeare after his strenuous feat of imaginatively exhausting all the guises of reality, knowing himself only to the extent of his becoming in his soul each of his dramatic creations, dying and having the following exchange with God:

> "I who have been so many men in vain want to be one and myself." The voice of the Lord answered from a whirlwind: "Neither am I anyone; I have dreamt the world as you dreamt your work, my Shakespeare, and among the forms in my dream are you, who like myself are many and no one."
> ("Everything and Nothing")

The difference in expectations of the two writers is vividly illustrated if Borges's cool appraisal of life is read against Barth's self-conscious conclusion to "Title," a not unsimilar exploration of the problem of authorial identity:

> Oh God comma I abhor self-consciousness. I despise what we have come to; I loathe our loathsome loathing, our place our time our situation, our loathesome art, this ditto necessary story. The blank of our lives. It's about over. Let the *denouement* be soon and unexpected, painless if possible, quick at least, above all soon. Now now! How in the world will it ever

And on this ironically self-conscious note of hopeless inconclusiveness Barth ceases, leaving us with the inescapable fact that the future is a blank, indeed has always been a blank except to adherents of a value system, which indirectly defines them as well as the future.

Grounded in the psychological reality of man rather than in the philosophical ideality of the world, Barth is using the *roman à clef* in *Lost in the Funhouse* as a parodic means of defining his role as person and of justifying his activity as author; but one must not forget that Barth is a master parodist, experimenting with ways of expressing the same skeptical view of things that is Borges's, only in the more difficult terms of person rather than of place, of the dizzying whorls of psyche rather than of the vertiginous spirals of space. Gerhard Joseph does not always keep this fact in mind. The result is that his commentary is forever blurring the distinction between author and persona. In the Maryland stories this mistake is understandable, since the author invites the reader to sympathize with his struggles to control an excessive and intractable language and an inadequate form to the exhaustion of means and the denial of ends that is Barth's parodic goal.

The funhouse is an elegant figure of speech, especially in its combination of local color realism and of Black Humor pluralism; but its designedly self-conscious exploration of sensibility disappoints its author's high hopes of "hinting to the reader things of which the narrator is unaware" or of casting "further and subtler lights upon the things it describes, sometimes ironically qualifying the more evident sense of the comparison." The mirror room can only reflect the appearance of the person presented to it, in this instance a thirteen-year-old adolescent still shaky on the significance of his sexual being. The world lies all before him, few memories behind him. The story admits as much when it diverts Ambrose from the mirror room and loses him in "some new or old part of the place that's not supposed to be used." Instead of winding "around on itself . . . like the snakes on Mercury's caduceus," Ambrose's perception moves outward, peeks through a seam between plyboard wall panels into a tool room where a man sits nodding on a stool, and finally, comfortingly, fantasies his future sexual certainties as husband and father. Nor is it as acceptable a resolution as Gerhard Joseph thinks[24] for Barth as authorial narrator to find in the "many distorted perspectives" of Ambrose the "barely disguised reflection" of his own "troubled psyche," and in the "lifelong entrapment" of Ambrose "within the labyrinth of his mind's making" a rationale for his own decision to "construct funhouses for others and be their secret operator—though he would rather be among the lovers for whom funhouses are designed." Especially questionable as device is this foisting onto Ambrose as adolescent the sophisticated rationalizations and fictional problem-solving of Barth as middle-aged author. "Lost in the Funhouse" is an Ocean City reverie that spins a psychological web of romanticized make-believe distressingly distant from the realism of the setting and from the facts of Barth's own life. A measure of its sentimentality is the closeness with which it skirts the vulgarisms of *Ah, Wilderness!* Barth, like Ambrose— like all of us—finds himself in this century to have strayed as both lover and designer into a funhouse; but that "insight" does not "wind around on itself like a whelk shell" leading him ever deeper into self-knowledge. The metaphor of funhouse and mirror room do not contain residual unknown ontological truths as at first they might seem to. As Ambrose notes despairingly when he watches himself refract into several "other persons": "In the funhouse mirror-room you can't see yourself go on forever, because no matter how you stand, your head gets in the way. Even if you had a glass periscope, the image of your eye would cover up the thing you really wanted to see." The funhouse is one of those clever fictional conceptions, an inventive objective correlative, of a pointless universe that one occasionally encounters in Black Humor. Drawn from a gimcrack American ethos, it fails to suggest "that imminence of a revelation that is not yet produced" ("The Wall and the Books") so mysteriously intrinsic to Borges's *ficciones* and parables.

In "Echo" Barth returns to the rich suggestiveness of archetypes and classical mythology. Not the hero of a thousand faces but Narcissus is seized upon for persona. In that mortal's flight from Echo (who "lives for her lovely lies" as others "live for the lie of love") toward self-love, Barth recognizes the plight of the twentieth-century storyteller, whose need to conceive himself through his tale is no less great than his will to tell the tale. Unfortunately one subverts the other. As with the masturbatory innocence of Narcissus ("who perishes by denying all except himself"), the "Overmuch presence" of the author drives him away from the possession of reality into a similar self-reflecting pool of self-destruction. The contrary model is Echo who "persists by effacing herself absolutely." The solution then, as Theban Tiresias is made to advise, is to cure self-absorption with saturation: "telling the story over as though it were another's until like a much-repeated word it loses sense." "Echo" is just such an exercise in saturation: the author retelling the myth of Narcissus and Echo in the form of Narcissus reciting his story to Tiresias, a true fabular *regressus in infinitum* (an author reciting about an author reciting about himself) in which Narcissus's death must "be partial as his self-knowledge," for "the voice persists, persists . . . goes on."

And yet: "Can it be believed?" the narrator asks, turning the story into a denial of itself. Can multiplication wind us back to the incontrovertible source of our being? Is there any finality to the infinity of possibilities? Even that question lacks a fixed point of reference but jostles as one possibility among myriad others. In yet one more recapitulation of his story, Barth remarks:

> Tiresias has gone astray; a voice not impossibly his own has bewildered him. The story of Narcissus, Tiresias, Echo is being repeated. It's alleged that Narcissus has wearied of himself and yearns to love another; on Tiresias's advice he employs the third person to repeat his tale as the seer does, until it loses meaning. No use: his self objectified's the more enthralling, like his blooming image in the spring. In vain Tiresias's cautions that the nymph may be nothing altruistic, but the soul of guile and sleight-of-tongue. Who knows but what her love has changed to mock? What she gives back as another's speech may be entire misrepresentation; especially ought one to beware what she chooses to repeat concerning herself. No use, no use: Narcissus grows fond; she speaks his language; Tiresias reflects that after all if one aspires to concern one's fatal self with another, one had as well commence with the nearest and readiest. Perhaps, he'll do the same: be beguiled with Narcissus out of knowledge of himself; listen silent as his voice goes on.
>
> Thus we linger forever on the autognostic verge—not you and I, but Narcissus, Tiresias, Echo. Are they still in the Thespian cave? Have they come together in the spring? Is Narcissus addressing Tiresias, Tiresias Narcissus? Have both expired?

The simultaneous affirmation and denial of an ultimate voice and hence persistent identity intimated by the myth of Narcissus and Echo is reiterated by the final two stories of *Lost in the Funhouse*. In "Menelaid," Barth retells with marvelous verve the effort of Menelaus to learn from Proteus on the shore at Pharos the secret of Helen's love. It was inevitable that Barth's preoccupation with the disguises masking identity from its own recognition should lead him to this myth, one of the two great expositions in western literature

37

(the other is of Joseph, Mary, and the annunciation) of man's faith in the fidelity of love and the persistence of self. A tour de force in narrative exhaustion of points of view, the story holds in balance seven voices as Menelaus imagines his yarning to Telemachus and Peisistratus about his imagining Helen hearing Proteus hearing Proteus's daughter Eidothea hearing Menelaus relate the story of the fall of Troy and his "recollection" of Helen. Through all the "layered sense" comes the reiterated word " ' " ' " ' " "Love!" ' " ' " ' " the cry that Helen loves only him, has never loved anyone but him, and that she has "languished . . . chaste and comfy" through all the years of the Trojan War out of harm's way at Pharos with Egyptian Proteus. But Barth's Menelaus has a modern sensibility. He cannot accept such a miraculous explanation, the imp of doubt gives him no peace. How is he to espouse her, he wonders, as lover? advocate? husband? "Who am I?" he asks and is answered through the multi-layers of voice: " ' " ' " ' " " ' " ' " ' ". Helen's history confirms for him his "grown conviction that the entire holocaust at Troy, with its prior and subsequent fiascos, was but a dream of Zeus's conjure" and his growing willingness to entertain the possibility "that Proteus somewhere on the beach became Menelaus holding the Old man of the Sea, Menelaus ceased." Both the irreverent slanginess of the parody and the multiple removes from reality of the points of view reiterate this skepticism. The only certainty clung to is the notion of the archetypal persistence of love. Nothing more survives, not Menelaus's voice, not the author's. All else, "Place and time, doer, done-to have lost their sense." Only the instinct of love persists: "when as must at last every tale, all tellers, all told, Menelaus's story itself in ten or ten thousand years expires, yet I'll survive it, I, in Proteus's terrifying last disguise, Beauty's spouse's odd Elysium: the absurd, unending possibility of love." The trouble with this solution to the sought for source of identity is that Menelaus's role as storyteller is not intrinsic to his nature but derives from a device of narrative. With the last story of the collection Barth corrects this "flow" in fictional conception.

In "Anonymiad" Barth merges myth and reality, the private dream of writer and the social world of reader, and both sexual and imaginative aspects of the life force, by scurrilously marrying the bard turned writer of prose successively to the nine muses. The

"Anonymiad" is a comic epic in prose, scatological, inelegant, parodying the hesitant inept first essays at literary devices subsequently in the history of western literature become convention. Its author is a rustic goatherder turned minstrel, a Homeric-like social climber who has ambitiously beguiled his way to the position of Acting Chief Minstrel (and spy) at Agamemnon's court, before being tricked ashore on a deserted island for life by Clytemnestra and Aegisthus. Left with nine amphorae of wine, he systematically over the years has used the jugs three ways: drunk their contents, "made each the temporary mistress of his sole passion," and stuffed them again with his fiction.

> Stranded by my foes,
> Nowadays I write in prose,
> Forsaking measure, rhyme, and honeyed diction;
>
> Amphora's my muse:
> When I finish off the booze,
> I hump the jug and fill her up with fiction.

In this wise he has wedded himself to each of the nine muses in turn, filling each jug with the seed of his loins and of his imagination. Thus freighted he has cast them into the sea (for Ambrose, the author as adolescent, to pluck from the water centuries later). Calliope, the ninth amphora, is slated to receive the last of his tales, the "Anonymiad," an epic tale in prose of the minstrel's life, as the cap to his previous poetical inventions of events of the Trojan War and its aftermath with which he had freighted the first eight amphorae. The "Anonymiad" is an exercise in circularity as much as in *regressus in infinitum*, a story about how the story came to be, about "a nameless minstrel" writing a tale about himself writing a tale, for an inconceivable reader—it and "all its predecessors . . . a continuing, strange love letter" in which the word has become everything—and nothing. The story is a paradigm for our time of ontological insecurity, of the anonymity of self, and of the unlikelihood even of the persistence of the individual voice. Thus has Barth fabled himself back through the literary perspectives of his bardic predecessors to the first recorded efforts of western man to define who he is and how his essential being has been moved ultimately by love? lust? the life force? the word? and to his recognition that even that instinct is reduced finally to the chance coincidence of the word with a reader.

The stories in *Lost in the Funhouse* represent alternative instances, realistic and mythic, of the author seeking to experience himself as an individual in relation to his creation of fictions. In George and Anastasia's triumph over WESCAC Barth had offered a hesitant affirmation of a kind of Jungian life force. Descending into the Belly "arsy-turvy—like two shoes in a box," they form a Yang-Yin of wholeness; but their sexual union and short-circuiting of WESCAC, while mystically certifying George as Grand Tutor, is so broadly comical in its parodic contrivances that it qualifies the affirmation. Barth has no illusions about having fashioned here an all seasonal potion for Global Village man, an elixir that will wend him back to the essence of his being. Love figures too extensively in Barth's stories as the source of anarchy and chaos, beginning with the Trojan War, brought up to date in the dynastic intrigues of Colonial America, and rendered on computer tape at West Campus. Nor does Barth have any illusions about our ability to achieve ontological security. In *Lost in the Funhouse* he transcends the agonizing efforts at self-definition of Ebenezer, Burlingame, and George Goat-Boy, and the equally traumatic biographies of the Maryland tales, and comes to rest in the serene Borgian acceptance of an identity that has no confirmatory existence apart from its fictional entity. Indeed, the mark of Borges's "The Immortal" is everywhere impressed in Barth's paradigmatic renderings of the myths of Narcissus, Menelaus, and the archetypal poet anonymous. His skeptical acceptance of the permanence of multiplicity, of even the possibility that one's self is but the dream of another insubstantial being, becomes the only viable strategy for confronting the Great Labyrinth, both human and cosmic. In parody alone may the artist hope to find a successive form that dissemblingly confirms continuation in time. To retell the old myths, to come paradigmatically ever closer to a great contemporary like Borges (as these stories so patently do), and to lampoon the anti-Gutenberg cries of McLuhan and company (as the stories also do) is to maintain the fiction of continuity and the reality of person in the limited persistence of the word, is finally, if nothing else, to give aesthetic validity to life.

NOTES TO CHAPTER II

1. "Humor with a Mortal Sting," *New York Times Book Review*, LXIX, pt. 2 (September 27, 1964), p. 60.

2. "The American Absurd Novel," *The World of Black Humor*, ed. Douglas M. Davis (New York, 1967), p. 309.

3. John Enck, "John Barth: An Interview," *Wisconsin Studies in Contemporary Literature*, VI (1965), 5.

4. "*Lolita*: The Springboard of Parody," *Wisconsin Studies in Contemporary Literature*, VIII (1967), 237.

5. "The Literature of Exhaustion," *The Atlantic*, CCXX (August, 1967), 29–34. Borges has written that "the Baroque is that style which deliberately exhausts (or tries to exhaust) its possibilities and borders on its own caricature" (quoted in *Labyrinths* [Norfolk, 1962], p. xxii).

6. Douglas M. Davis, *The World of Black Humor*, p. 30.

7. John Barth, "The Literature of Exhaustion," p. 34.

8. Cf. John Wain's review of *Beautiful Losers*, "Making It Now," in *New York Review of Books* (April 28, 1966), p. 18.

9. As articulated by Brown in *Life Against Death* and *Love's Body*. Robert Boyers, "Attitudes toward Sex in American 'High Culture,'" *Annals of the American Academy of Political and Social Science*, CCCLXXVI (1968), 209–210.

10. "Humor with a Mortal Sting," p. 61.

11. Hart Crane, "The Wine Menagerie," l. 29.

12. John Barth, "The Literature of Exhaustion," p. 29.

13. William Wordsworth, *The Prelude*, X, 923.

14. Gerhard Joseph, *John Barth* (Minneapolis, 1970), p. 39. Joseph's study in one of the University of Minnesota Pamphlets on American Writers (No. 91) is the best discussion of Barth I know of. I am gratefully indebted to it in my remarks on Barth here, even though I disagree with Joseph on more than one count, most particularly his ready acceptance of Barth's McLuhanesque professions about his art such as the "Author's Note" to *Lost in the Funhouse*. A chronological view of Barth's development (which is Joseph's) inadvertently roots Barth in a psychological and a genetic realism, from which perspective the critic only with difficulty can accommodate the comedy of Barth's most recent parodic ventures.

15. "John Barth: An Interview," *Wisconsin Studies in Contemporary Literature*, VI (1965), 12.

16. R. D. Laing, *The Divided Self* (Baltimore, 1960), pp. 41, 43.

17. Erich Fromm, *The Sane Society* (New York, 1955), pp. 114, 124.

18. Joseph, *John Barth*, p. 37.

19. *Ibid.*, p. 29.

20. *Ibid.*, p. 38.

21. "John Barth: An Interview," *Wisconsin Studies in Contemporary Literature*, VI (1965), 12.

22. The Baudelairean line reads, "—Hypocrite lecteur,—mon semblable, —mon frère!" T. S. Eliot's adaptation of the line in "The Game of Chess," *The Waste Land* ("You! hypocrite lecteur!—mon semblable,—mon frère!") is closer to Barth's outburst.

23. Cf. below, chapter 4.

24. *John Barth*, pp. 39–40.

III

THE UNSENSING OF THE SELF; AND, THE UNCONFIRMED THESIS OF KURT VONNEGUT

I

In the logical world of Judeo-Greco-Christian values—the pre-McLuhan world as some with a flair for Madison Avenue tags now like to remark—the underpinnings of *non sequitur* and *post hoc, ergo propter hoc* provided support for the intellectual structures of Aristotle, St. Thomas Aquinas, Freud, and Marx. No such principles are available in the pluralistic world. The conventionally coherent literary structure becomes patently impossible, the traditional form a defective ordering of alien complexities, its configuration dissociated from its content. The Black Humor writer inhabiting this new atomistic world has an obvious option. He can write incredibly omnibus parodies of knowledge, which attempt to master the labyrinth of an illogical world by exhausting every twist and turn and blind alley in it. In practical terms this strategy is transparently impossible, as Barth's heroic efforts in this direction only too readily argue. A workable alternative for the Black Humorist is to hold a limited number of viewpoints in equipoise, as literary counterparts of a world devoid of a discursive value system. We have a radical version of such a procedure when the narrative and surface details refuse to verify the plot, undercutting its thematic statement with a contrary set of referents. This is the strategy Barth is feeling his way toward (despite his counter urge for completeness) in *The Sot-Weed Factor*, *Giles Goat-Boy*, and the late stories especially of *Lost in the Funhouse*.

One can find traces of this thematic pluralism in fiction as far back as the Romantics—but with one all-important difference. In *The Heart of Midlothian*, for example, Scott presents what might be defined as such a pluralistic view of the nature of justice and of the legal code. It is clear though that the narrative plan of the novel does not develop out of a conscious philosophy of absurdity, but is the inadvertent result of Scott's abstract belief in the social and moral efficacy of the law coming into conflict with his human recognition of the harsh inefficacy of a single statute. Reluctance to judge even a patently inadequate portion of the law leads him to equivocate, leads him to send Jeanie Deans to London to seek redress through personal means rather than legal. The saving of Effie Deans from execution for a crime she did not commit becomes a question of individual mercy rather than of judicial probity. Thus Effie lives. The statute stands. And Scott, who appears to be viewing the problem of justice from multiple vantage points, never actually calls the law into question, never outright asks about the unerring ability of the law to discriminate between innocence and guilt.

The Romantics are men reflecting in unconscious ways a pluralistic vision of the world, while still holding doggedly onto a unitive conception of man and the world. Hence, in an imaginative construct like Coleridge's *The Rime of the Ancient Mariner* one encounters a disjunction between the poet's expressed optimism that nature has sacramental wholeness and his subconscious fear that caprice rather than order prevails in the universe.[1] Yet the latter response remains a latent expression of the poet's unconfessed thoughts and emotions; its irony is unplanned, its ambivalence inadvertent, an unwilled disclosure of soul, rather than a formulated metaphysics of dissonance. In much Black Humor fiction this dissonance has become a conscious generative part of the grammar of theme and form.

Such a strategy flirts dangerously with the reduction of the fictional form to what at best may be an uncomfortable inconclusiveness and at worse an atomistic rendering of disorderly experience. Indicative of how academic are the alternatives available to these writers, however, is Borges's decision not to revise the title of his essay "A New Refutation of Time," even though he was "not un-aware that it is an example of the monster termed by the logicians *contradictio in adjecto*, because stating that a refutation of time is new (or old) attributes to it a predicate of temporal nature which establishes the very notion the subject would destroy." "I leave it as it is," he adds, "so that its slight mockery may prove that I do not exaggerate the importance of these verbal games. Besides, our lan-guage is so saturated and animated by time that it is quite possible there is not one statement in these pages which in some way does not demand or invoke the idea of time." Perhaps out of the interplay of part-truth and error, Borges hopes, truth may have a better chance to emerge than out of normative modes of thought. Such are the desperate shifts to which one kind of novelist in the sixties has been forced by his honest response to the existential implications of the times.

II

The novels of Kurt Vonnegut are a case in point. Their seeming artlessness, especially in their pluralistic handling of form and theme, tended for years to put readers off as not worth one's serious attention. He was forced to write pot boilers and slick short stories, to teach on an itinerant basis, to forego hard-bound publication in favor of pulp paperback distribution, in short, to turn his hand to whatever literary shift might earn a living. Not until the unexpected success of *Slaughterhouse-Five* did he emerge from an underground reputation kept alive by college generations and academic circles to public visibility in *Life Magazine*. It is no exaggeration to say that his audience has been slow in learning how to read his stories.

The reception of *God Bless You, Mr. Rosewater* strikingly illus-trates this obtuseness. The novel adopts the strategies of the un-confirmed thesis with such effectiveness that it has frequently been misread either as a sentimentally botched reworking of the parable of the Good Samaritan or as a randomly conceived Utopian nar-rative which takes pot shots at everything under the sun in modern America.[2]

God Bless You, Mr. Rosewater ostensibly updates the argument for the Christian ethic that one should love his fellow man. It posits the overwhelming need for such love in a technological age, which increasingly relegates humans to an obsolescent category, substituting efficient machines for defective individuals. It suggests that Christ's consort with publicans and prostitutes has taken on fresh meaning with the growing number of humans rendered useless by our computerized civilization. And it indicts an obsession with wealth, which has undermined the American experiment, vitiating the American pioneering independence of action and judgment, until wealth has become identified with sloth (Stewart Buntline), lesbianism (Amanita Buntline), homosexuality (Bunny Weeks), drunkenness (Caroline Rosewater), pornography (Lila Buntline), and death (Fred Rosewater, who sells insurance with the philosophy that the value of life lies in the worth of death). In short, the novel acridly maintains, the American dream of a new Eden with a new Adam, possible in the virgin wilderness of a new land, has materialized into a junk yard by way of the glories of technology. In support of its Samaritan thesis, it holds up Eliot Rosewater as the ideal of the millionaire turned Do-Gooder (a sort of post-World War II Andrew Carnegie), a modern re-enactment of Christ-like commitment of more than money—of self—to the poor in body and spirit.

Yet, in its characterization of Eliot Rosewater, in its description of his Indiana utopia, in its parodies, its imagery and symbolism, its tone and structure, the novel asks us to question its moral stance. Even the title is a stand-off, with the first half ("God Bless You, Mr. Rosewater") reminding us of Christ's teachings on love, and the second half ("Or Pearls Before Swine") reiterating the Sermon on the Mount's warning against wasting the gift of the Kingdom of Heaven on those who will not enter it.[3]

The tone of *infra dig* is pronounced in the Biblical allusions, which one would expect to confirm the Samaritan theme but which contrariwise work as often as not to cast doubt on its validity and to cast jibes at the idea of Jesus *redivivus*. Eliot's parody of the Biblical "begats" in his history of the Rosewater family points up the inadequacy of the American dream of equality, fraternity, and trust in God. The genealogy of the Rosewater males, from Noah ("a humorless, constipated Christian farm boy") to Lister (Eliot's father, who "has spent nearly the whole of his adult life in the

Congress of the United States, teaching morals"), is a dreary litany of how puritanical industry and capitalistic democracy realize not a utopia of *E pluribus unum* under one God and one President, but an aristocracy of the wealthy committed humorlessly, in non working hours, to the exploitive patronage of the arts and the "spiritual elevation of the poor . . . on Sundays" (pp. 19–21).

Not even the latter-day Samaritan, Eliot Rosewater, however, escapes the scornful lash of the parody. Unlike the generations of the sons of the Biblical Noah, which culminate in the patriarch Abraham, the generations of the sons of the Indiana Noah end with Eliot, "a drunkard, a Utopian dreamer, a tinhorn, an aimless fool," who begat "not a soul" (pp. 22–23). In the generations of the Rosewaters, the humanitarian motives of the Good Samaritan have transmigrated to the Americas, turned inside out and diagnosed as a neurotic illness, Samaritrophia, "*hysterical indifference to the troubles of those less fortunate than oneself*," which is cured by arousing "Enlightened Self-interest" (p. 54). Eliot appears as both a Jesus and a Jonah figure. Like Christ, who consorted with publicans and prostitutes, Eliot chooses to befriend misfits and drunks. He also manages to practice the New Testament injunction against cleaving to father and mother and family. But Eliot's neglect of his wife, leading to her nervous breakdown, plus his unconcern for her plight, remakes him less in the image of Christ than in the antic witlessness of disposition of Diana Moon Glampers, one of the unloved whom he succors. His sublimely mad efforts to "save" a county economically ravaged by his forebears are repeatedly presented in terms that could be judged both inadequate and disreputable, ludicrously so. To cite one of many instances, his final ploy in the story. The innocent correspondent in a paternity suit, he orders his lawyer to draw up papers "that will legally acknowledge that every child in Rosewater County said to be mine [all told, there are fifty-seven claimants] *is* mine, regardless of blood type. Let them all have full rights of inheritance as my sons and daughters. . . . And tell them that their father loves them, no matter what they may turn out to be. . . . And tell them . . . to be fruitful and multiply" (p. 217). Eliot's directive here to the recipients of his charity is almost obscene in the context of the current crisis of overpopulation, which the novel explicitly brings to our attention in its concern for the growing num-

47

bers of useless people on earth. The identification, furthermore, of Eliot with God and God's directive to man to people the earth (Eliot is also dressed in white tennis clothes and waves his racket "as though it were a magic wand") is rendered questionable by Eliot's impotency.

Eliot's love (caritas) for mankind is slyly laughed at in other ways—as in the epigraph to the novel: *"The Second World War was over* [Eliot Rosewater is speaking]—*and there I was at high noon, crossing Times Square with a Purple Heart on"*—where Eliot's capacity for self-sacrifice is ironically deflated by the pun on his aroused sexuality, the deflation intensified by our subsequently learning of his impotency. The emotional bankruptcy of Eliot's effort to love all men indiscriminately is succinctly articulated by his father:

> "Eliot did to the word *love* what the Russians did to the word *democracy*. If Eliot is going to love everybody, no matter what they are, no matter what they do, then those of us who love particular people for particular reasons had better find ourselves a new word." He looked up at an oil painting of his deceased wife. "For instance—I loved *her* more than I loved our garbage collector, which makes me guilty of the most unspeakable of modern crimes: *Dis-crim-i-nay-tion.*" (p. 79)

Senator Rosewater, of course, is confusing eros with caritas; still, the Senator's complaint carries conviction, for to love everybody willy-nilly is to love no one in reality.

Eliot as humanitarian is also downgraded through the parallel with his second cousin, Fred Rosewater. Like Eliot, Fred sees himself as in the business of saving souls. He creates "sizable estates" for widows and orphans by selling life insurance policies. Grateful women address him, as they do Eliot, in the heartfelt terms "God bless you, Mr. Rosewater" (p. 122). If Eliot works his miracles sitting on a toilet in an abandoned dental office, Fred conducts his business on a stool at the coffee counter of a newsstand. The cash nexus of both men's philanthropy, played down in the references to Eliot but confirmed by his considering the recipients of his charity to be his "clients" (p. 169), becomes pervasively evident in Fred's comings and goings. Indeed, Eliot's ministry to the castoffs, drunkards, and misfits of Rosewater County is invariably calculated in small sums of money, euphemistically entered in a ledger as Fellowships. When compared to Christ's personal ministry, Eliot's utopian experiment appears gratuitously impersonal and capricious. He solicits the indigent in hit-and-miss fashion with stickers, *"Don't Kill Yourself. Call the Rosewater Foundation"* (p. 90), pasted in every phone booth in the county and on the cars of volunteer firemen, and he mostly communicates with the needy over the telephone. The useless types to whom he has become patron saint include such unsavory criminals and mental defectives as a psychotic wife killer and a demented Nazi—hardly characteristic instances of technological obsolescence. His dispensation of "grace" to the Rosewater community takes such bizarre forms as his purchasing for the town fire station "the main air-raid siren of Berlin during the Second World War"—"To the best of Eliot's knowledge . . . the loudest alarm in the Western Hemisphere" (p. 92).

One of the most telling arguments against our accepting Eliot's "Christ-like" actions at face value is the psychological explanation given for his love of mankind. On one level of the novel's statement, Eliot is portrayed as a man in desperate need of electric shock treatment. His mental afflictions range from hypochondria—his medicine cabinet is "crammed with vitamins and headache remedies and hemorrhoid salves and laxatives and sedatives" (p. 63)—to paranoia. When Mary Moody, a Rosewater County resident dependent on Eliot's philanthropy, erroneously phones him on the fire department hot line, he screams, "God *damn* you for calling this number. You should go to jail and rot! Stupid sons of bitches who make personal calls on a fire department line should go to hell and fry forever!" A few seconds later, the sobbing Mary Moody calls back on the Rosewater Foundation phone. All sweetness and light, Eliot asks, "What on earth is the trouble, dear?" And Vonnegut adds, "He honestly didn't know. He was ready to kill whoever had made her cry" (p. 172). The saintly fool of Dostoievsky's fiction has deteriorated badly.

Eliot is obsessed with the belief that firemen are "the only examples of enthusiastic unselfishness to be seen in this land" (p. 211). They are associated with his childhood happiness, when he was mascot of a Fire Department; but firemen also arouse strong guilt feelings in him, because he had mistakenly killed three unarmed German firemen during the war. He was subsequently hospitalized for combat fatigue. Linked in his mind with this guilt is his responsibility for the death of his mother. Although an expert sailor, he jibbed unexpectedly one day when he had taken her for a sail, the "slashing boom" knocking her overboard whereupon she "sank like a stone" (p. 38). To escape his mental demons, Oresteian and otherwise, he has become a drunkard and patron of firemen as well as a celibate. He is "deeply touched by the idea of an inhabited planet with an atmosphere that was eager to combine violently with almost everything the inhabitants held dear. He was speaking of Earth and the element oxygen." Firemen loom large for him, therefore, as a "band of brothers" joined in the "*humane* thing" of "keeping our food, shelter, clothing and loved ones from combining with oxygen" (pp. 31–32).

Fire clearly has a sexual significance for Eliot. Unlike the pyromaniac bent on starting fires for the sake of sexual arousal, however, Eliot, who views sexual excitement as "irrelevant" (p. 84), is bent on dousing fires. This emotional fixation is strikingly illustrated by his guilt feelings—"those of a weak-willed puritan with respect to pornography" (p. 200)—about a book he owns, *The Bombing of Germany*. He is afraid of being caught reading it. A passage in the book describing the fire-bombing of Dresden makes his palms sweat. Eliot's fixation with firemen is expressive of his impotence, of his suppression of sexuality, and of his transference of sexual energies to the creation of utopia. Thus a psychoanalyst retained by Senator Rosewater diagnoses Eliot's illness! And thus surely Vonnegut means us to understand Eliot's humanitarian hangup. Even Eliot's dress betrays his deflection of the sex drive. He rattles around his office "swaddled in the elephant wrinkles of warsurplus long underwear" (p. 62), a giant in Dr. Denton's! A like expression of his illness is his flight from direct involvement with individuals, underscored by his communication with recipients of his philanthropy over the telephone and by Vonnegut's identification of him with Hamlet (cf. pp. 41, 60).

To offer "a booze problem" (p. 59) and sexual delusion as the psychological rationale for Eliot's emulation of the Good Samaritan is to contradict the narrative affirmation of the novel. To define Eliot's altruism in such aberrative terms is to compromise his

Christian motives, and, ultimately, to question the validity of three thousand years of Judeo-Christian assumptions. No less under a cloud of suspicion is the theme of social and economic utopia that is developed in conjunction with the Christian theme of brotherly love in the novel. Indeed, one may go a step farther and say that the general strategy of the novel is to pose the problem of the obsolete man in a technological society, weighing the various kinds of love, puritan ideals of industry, and social theories of welfare which have always in the past sustained and succored man, while carefully refraining from any normative judgment. In this respect *God Bless You, Mr. Rosewater* is a thoroughly pluralistic novel. It exhausts the types and categories of human regard for their kind in the characters of Eliot, Sylvia, and Senator Rosewater and their progenitors, Harry Pena and sons, Lila Buntline, Bunny Weeks and Amanita Buntline, Stewart Buntline and his ancestors, Fred and Caroline Rosewater, old McAllister, Selena Deal and Wilfred Parrot, Kilgore Trout, and Norman Mushari. Nowhere in this "debate," though, does it single out which kind of love will answer man's current needs. The novel refuses to resolve or to confirm any of its premises.

III

A key question raised by Vonnegut concerns the constitution of reality. If traditional cultural systems have lost their perspicuity, what does man do for a sense of purpose in life? If he is a Vonnegut, a Pynchon, a Nabokov, a Barth, a Borges, he does like Eliot Rosewater and Billy Pilgrim, he re-invents himself and his universe.[4] With Tralfamadorian logic he dispenses with *why* in favor of *what*. Novels which are the product of such thought as often as not become outrageous re-creations of history—paradigms of reality, which cheerfully admit to being products of imaginative play without compromising their serious intentions of being the best enlargement and control of one's environment available.

This ontological incertitude echoes one of the intellectual crises of the last 250 years. In the eighteenth century, man took the first of successive steps leading him away from philosophically verifiable knowledge of the world he lives in. Lockean psychology, codified into associationist psychology as the century wore on, cut man off from the phenomenal world, forcing him, with ever increasing self-consciousness, to substitute the world of his mind for the unverifiable world of space and time. Despite their epistemological isolation, however, the Romantics never doubted the reality and viability of the self. The Victorians though found increasing difficulty in verifying even this "certainty," not only its affirmation of the self in relation to an evolving physical world but also—and here the age was provided with its intellectual crisis—in relation to what was always in the past assumed to be a fixed noumenal world. In our century, particularly in the past two decades, the self as a verifiable, definable, even possible, entity has vanished in the ironic acceptance of a world without metaphysical center, one fragmented into multiple realities. Nor does the astounding advance in phenomenal knowledge of the universe offer us as yet an alternative set of beliefs. Rather, the sciences tend increasingly to answer our request for understanding of our world in terms untranslatable into words. Consequently, as George Steiner has remarked, our disorientation now includes the additional anxiety for man-as-verbal-animal of silence, toward which Beckett has been tentatively exploring his way for decades, and in which Salinger seems already to have settled. We live in a world, the scientific descriptions of which are no longer communicable with verbal counters. The result, in the words of Maxine Greene, is that "we seem to be confronting a reality that is totally mysterious or devoid of meaning."[5]

The implications for artists—writers, painters, sculptors, composers—of this loss of faith in the meaningful reality of both the self and the world have been evocative of new artistic thrusts into areas of random and serial forms, considered by older aesthetics to be inartistic and unbeautiful. Tom Stoppard's extraordinary version of the Hamlet caper in his play *Rosencrantz and Guildenstern Are Dead*, as seen through the eyes of two "absurdists"—lineal descendants of Vladimir and Estragon—could only have been conceived in this century. Surely Rosencrantz and Guildenstern's disorientation—as also the strolling Players'—derives from the absence of any center to their worlds. The royal directive has disconcertingly abdicated from Rosencrantz and Guildenstern's frame of reference, as the audience has from the Players'. One might also characterize the conceptual shift of the American dream in the past decade from the nineteenth-century ideal of the melting pot to the contemporary ardor for ethnic pluralism, as part of a general cultural metamorphosis of the One into the Many, and of Future orientation into Now participation.

This emergent world view is corroborated by the directions taken recently in the arts other than literature. As early as 1949 in the painting *Attic*, Willem de Kooning had begun to treat his subject dualistically. Andrew Forge, analyzing this picture, comments that "almost every bounding line reads two ways, however spontaneously drawn, so that in the very act of isolating and identifying form, the negative shape against which one reads it becomes itself a positive shape with a rival identity of its own."[6] Similarly, one can read a second face in the breasts, belly, and pelvis of many of de Kooning's women of the fifties, parodying the bashed and battered true face. Or does the parody call into question what one conventionally considers the facial part of the anatomy? And in de Kooning's 1968–69 show at Knoedler's, his studies of women, sunnier and more flippant than those slashed, smashed, punched, flattened, and dismembered females of the fifties, now embrace both day-dream and nightmare, both desire and fear. Eve or Lilith, as one critic notes, is also "in her new disguise . . . Candy or Barbarella."[7] With such "both/ and" visions of universal woman, de Kooning parallels the positive/ negative versions of reality of Vonnegut, and the matter/ antimatter molecular systems of some contemporary scientists.

The *oeuvres* of two other artists—the sculptor Robert Smithson and the composer John Cage—are neat nonverbal equivalents of the Black Humor penchant for giving an air of contingency to otherwise carefully rendered structures. Smithson's "non-sites" and Cage's "scoring" for radios are self-repudiating reconstructions of myth-making processes of thought. In their arrangements of the discrete, they wittily evade the puerility of single, ideal constructs.

"I want to de-mythify things," to take "away the vaulted mystery that is supposed to reside" in a system, Smithson has told an interviewer.[8] As with his recent *Franklin, New Jersey*, Smithson will choose an actual site. In this instance, on an aerial map of the city of Franklin, showing the distribution of ore deposits, he drew converging lines, intersected by parallel lines, which divided the area into five trapezoids of diminishing size. He then filled five wooden boxes, conforming to these trapezoids, with ore gathered from, and proportional in amount to, what is found at the site. These boxes he titled *Franklin, New Jersey.*

Both Smithson and Cage, in the parodic forms that their imposition of arbitrary systems on otherwise discrete materials takes, are satirizing the processes of thought by which they presume man orders his experience. Cage has carefully scored his composition *Piece for Six Radios* for specified radio dial settings at stipulated periods of time. This "arrangement" of radio stations guarantees that harmony and continuity will occur only at random intervals, and deliberately promotes in their stead unpredictable variation and multiplicity—for radio stations do not broadcast the same music every day, nor does every city have stations broadcasting on all the frequencies for which the piece is scored. Similarly, the trapezoidal boxes of diminishing size, in Smithson's *Franklin, New Jersey*, suggest an order and symmetry ironically denied by the arbitrariness of using boxes of special dimensions as representative of the site and by the distortion of substituting random chunks of ore collected from the area as descriptive of the terrain.

The preoccupation of contemporary artists with such strategies of self-repudiation was everywhere visible in the Whitney Museum's 1968 annual exhibition of sculpture. The traditional acceptance of the self as a reliable sensor was particularly under attack, the ambiguous line between object and image explored with a special note of urgent and anxious inventiveness. Six foot plexiglass prisms by Charles Ross, for example, disclosed not one's own expected reflection but other onlookers, distorted and edged in rainbow spectra, standing on the reverse side—the self displaced by multiple figures of otherness. The reality of the situation was further complicated by its remaining a moot question as to whether one was actually looking at other people or at an image of them. Working with a quite different set of means—with one hundred oval blips of plastic, hair, and wood scattered randomly about the museum—Richard Arschwager succeeded in forcing upon our attention the sinister unreliability of our senses when confronted by an unstructured protean experience. Best described as multiple forms of uncertain reality, suggestive of "both furry puppy dogs and giant leeches," according to *Time*, "combining sardonic playfulness with an unspoken

UNSENSING OF THE SELF

threat," [9] these blips were just as easily mistaken for humidifiers and dust filters.

In both these works, the preoccupation with the components of reality includes, as in much Black Humor, a resistance to confirmation of the object. The giant planks of John McCracken offer a variant formulation of this skepticism, which not incongruously contains an aura of mystery about its suspension of judgment. Leaning accidentally against a wall like carelessly forgotten totems, they have the shape of boards but the enameled gloss of metal automobile parts. To place this art in focus, so one can read it meaningfully, one must be ready to accept the possibility that the world is both a combination of all things and of nothing at all. This includes even that last-ditch epistemological makeshift, the human mind, which sustained man in the eighteenth and nineteenth centuries. It too becomes merely one random assemblage among many, rather than a unique creation. Hence, we have Frank Gallo's acidulous commentary, *Man with a Necktie* (in the 1968 Whitney show), a bust in glistening epoxy of masculine sartorial elegance—but with one self-denying defect, the Valentino handsome face is framed with flapping cupped ears like those staring out from the cover pages of *Mad* magazines. Similarly, the pride of *Homo sapiens*, conveyed in the confident stride and elegant bronze sheen of Ernest Trova's "Falling Man" studies, is compromised by armless, anatomically blank bodies, like nothing so much as showcase dummies, and by mechanical devices hanging from chest and back that question the full humanity of the figures.

IV

Some of the most searching art of the sixties is grappling with the nature of a world in which reality consists of arbitrary mental constructs and selfhood of unsought-for relationships. The position of much Black Humor fiction on this issue is aptly put by Bokonon, the mountebank prophet of Vonnegut's novel *Cat's Cradle*. In a parable on "the folly of pretending to discover, to understand," the nature and limits of God's design, Bokonon observes about an Episcopalian lady from Newport, Rhode Island, that "She was a fool, and so am I, and so is anyone who thinks he sees what God is Doing" (p. 15).

Failure to recognize or understand this cool, uninvolved contemplation of man's intellectual limitations has caused even such a perceptive critic as Frederick J. Hoffman to dismiss a book like Thomas Pynchon's *V.*, because "One of its principal faults is that it makes fun of the reasons why it makes fun of everything." [10]

One of the central ironies of *Cat's Cradle* is that through "the bittersweet lies" of the true-false religion Bokononism, the novel thematically quizzes itself. The first sentence in "The Books of Bokonon" states that "All of the true things I am about to tell you are shameless lies" (p. 16). And the narrator, himself a Bokononist, adds, "Anyone unable to understand how a useful religion can be founded on lies will not understand this book either" (p. 16). Given this "untruth" as the basis of all it purports to say truthfully about human experience, *Cat's Cradle* becomes an extended exercise in subversion. The title cheerfully warns us of the possible emptiness of its contents. Newt Hoenikker defines a cat's cradle thus: "nothing but a bunch of X's between somebody's hands, and little kids look and look and look at all those X's . . . *No damn cat, and no damn cradle*" (p. 137). The many names of the town of Bolivar and the multiple nationalities of the island of San Lorenzo slyly contradict the notion of identity—and hence of being. The unreality of delineating a person is succinctly illustrated by the contradictions in the character of Julian Castle, a Jungle medical missionary modeled on Albert Schweitzer, whose "saintly deeds" jostle disconcertingly with the cynicism of "the satanic things he thought and said" (p. 140). Not only is the narrator a convert to Bokononism, who confessedly believes in lies, but his information about the early life of Bokonon (when he was still the ragtail Negro adventurer Lionel Boyd Johnson) is gained from another "lying" Bokononist's manuscript, Philip Castle's history of San Lorenzo. The entire novel in a sense is a parody of "The Books of Bokonon," its short, page-length chapters, although not rendered in Bokonon's Calypso jingles, aping their quizzical cynicism—which further cautions us about accepting the narrative at face value.

The skepticism of *Cat's Cradle* calls into question even physical substance, the basic stuff of reality, which ordinarily represents for us the last word in stability. Dr. Hoenikker's discovery of ice-nine, which stacks and locks the atoms of liquid in a different, orderly way, so that water is frozen into a new rigid form, assumes that the molecular arrangement of matter, as we know it, is not pre-emptive of other possible arrangements. Whereas scientists have accepted for a long time such an open-ended world, having already isolated ice-one, ice-two, and ice-three, and admit the possibility of an undisclosed number of additional ice formations, the man on the street, secure in his almost medieval faith in the orderliness of nature, can only react with puzzlement and anxiety. *Cat's Cradle* forces him to face up to the radical instability of a world in which even the molecular structure of matter is potentially inconstant.

Cat's Cradle is a novel about the varieties of truth available to man: scientific, religious, political, social, economic, humanistic. Ultimately, in its presentation of the open-ended, unconfirmable dilemma of human knowledge and wisdom, the novel sardonically blurs veracity and falsehood, treating them as interchangeable for all practical human purposes. It refuses to confirm what is reality—neither what we say it is nor what it insists on being despite our words—nowhere more epigrammatically put than in the confession of the Bokononist narrator about "the cruel paradox of Bokononist thought, the heartbreaking necessity of lying about reality, and the heartbreaking impossibility of lying about it" (p. 223). To begin each chapter of this "Bokononist" novel with the mathematical symbol for a logical conclusion ($\therefore$) is to remind us slyly, insouciantly, of the unverifiability of knowledge.

That this quiz of "truth" is more than a clever novelistic device, is really expressive of Vonnegut's habitual turn of mind, is confirmed by his other novels, *Player Piano*, *The Sirens of Titan*, *Mother Night*, and most recently *Slaughterhouse-Five*.

In *Player Piano*, a case is made for social perfectibility. Management is portrayed as capable of spectacular success in elevating Mr. Averageman to a happy, healthy usefulness, the organization existing for his needs and tastes, not indifferent and aloof towards him. But the drab, monotonous life of the non-ruling laborers undercuts this comfortable notion with an assertion of the worth of men over machines and institutions. Even in this simple antithesis between the human and the mechanical, however, Vonnegut's praise of man is disturbingly unconfirmed. The Ghost Shirt Movement, pledged to destruction of the authoritarian machine-

57

dominated society and to restoration of a society of men, proves to be no less instinctively totalitarian. In engineering a Messiah, the Movement uses Paul Proteus as remorselessly as do the managerial elite. Equally distressing is the obtuseness of the survivors of the aborted Revolution, who having destroyed the machines begin to repair them out of pride and amusement, starting the process of recreating the system which will render them useless again. Thus the problem of stability posed by the novel in the form of such antitheses as spiritual needs versus material satisfactions and of human disorderliness versus machine-controlled regularity continues unresolved at the end.

A similar studied inconclusiveness characterizes the problem of means and ends demonstrated in the purposive random of the Tralfamadorian postal system in *The Sirens of Titan*. To get a message to an unidentified intergalactic destination, we are informed, the Great Wall of China was built, Stonehenge erected, thousands of years of earthling history enacted, millions of lives given birth to and delivered into death. And the message? A standard Western Union-like salutation: "Greetings."

Mother Night ostensibly explores the contemporary problems of guilt and identity, but with equally disquieting inconclusiveness, blandly suggesting the probable irrelevance of any answer we might conjugate to these important questions. "We are what we pretend to be," Vonnegut reminds us in an Introduction, "so we must be careful about what we pretend to be" (p. v)—a paradox which has the ring of truth. And the novel sets out to prove it. Both betrayer and betrayed, Howard W. Campbell, Jr., play-acts the American patriot-spy masquerading-as-Nazi until he cannot distinguish between his true self and his Doppleganger. His Nazi guise so confuses him that he finally sentences himself to death "for crimes against himself" (p. 202). In the rendering of this twentieth-century tragedy, which echoes more than one case familiar to newspaper readers of the past thirty years, Vonnegut dramatizes Campbell's apologia as a fabrication of the modern totalitarian mind unable to distinguish clearly between truth and falsity, while mitigating his offenses by portraying him as no worse than the rest of society and possibly better in that he accepts his burden of guilt. As a kind of reverse Eliot Rosewater, Campbell is first explicitly convicted of the heinous crime of aiding and abetting the Nazi extermination of the Jews, and then partly, and covertly, rehabilitated as a redemptive scapegoat of our time. Thus, in a larger sense, the novel is concerned with the multiple faces of truth. In an Editor's Note, Vonnegut suggests that the novel's thematic concern with the politics of self should not be swallowed uncritically, since these pages are Campbell's edited confessions and he was "a one-time playwright of moderate reputation." "To say that he was a writer," Vonnegut adds, "is to say that the demands of art alone were enough to make him lie, and to lie without seeing. . . . I will risk the opinion that lies told for the sake of artistic effect—in the theater, for instance, and in Campbell's confessions, perhaps—can be, in a higher sense, the most beguiling forms of truth" (p. ix). It is not accidental, probably, that most of Vonnegut's heroes—Campbell, Eliot Rosewater, Bokonon, John the narrator of *Cat's Cradle*—are artists *manqué*, underscoring Vonnegut's concern with the nature of appearance and the enigma of reality. Like *Cat's Cradle*, *Mother Night* refuses to pit truth against falsehood. It prefers to arrange its contradictory "truths" on parallel planes, forcing us to realize uneasily that the complexity of moral experience may differ in kind from the complexity of aesthetic experience. But on the question of a final disposition of this grid of possibilities, as on the questions of Campbell's guilt and his identity, the novel withholds ultimate confirmation.

The motor that drives *Slaughterhouse-Five* is Vonnegut's fixation with the firebombing of Dresden during World War II. The condemnation of the bombing—Vonnegut calls it a massacre—is developed thematically into a sturdy protest against killing. "I have told my sons," Vonnegut writes in the Preface, "that they are not under any circumstances to take part in massacres, and that the news of massacres of enemies is not to fill them with satisfaction or glee" (p. 17). At the same time, however, the Tralfamadore subplot singles out the earthling concept of death as a silly misapprehension based on a linear view of time. According to Tralfamadorian knowledge, no one ever dies, but is alive somewhere in that living moment, hence "the negligibility of death" (p. 164). If the novel's most bitter gambit is that we are all, like Billy Pilgrim, "on the way to the Slaughterhouse" (p. 168) by virtue of one or the other of man's ingenious devices for self-destruction, then its counter move is reflected in the Tralfamadorian saying, "So it goes," uttered with ceremonious cosmic sanctimony at every mention or instance of death. Indeed, the multiple instances of human demise and its variety of forms as chronicled in the novel, plus the historical emphasis on death as the inevitable conclusion to life, transforms the fictional statement into a modern version of the eternal Dance of Death, which further qualifies the narrow perspective of Vonnegut's opening remarks as author that he is writing an indictment of war. As Vonnegut admits, an anti-war book is as senseless as "an anti-*glacier* book" (p. 3). Billy Pilgrim is less the embodiment of every soldier led to slaughter to the tune of fife and drum than Everyman (as civilian, since he is never fully outfitted with military garb, even in the Battle of the Bulge) whose pilgrimage, unlike John Bunyan's hero's progress toward the celestial city, steps pointlessly toward the void. To complain about the inevitability of death, however, is to shift the grounds of one's argument, is to discuss the subject of slaughter-by-war in a comic frame of reference.

V

In none of his novels does Vonnegut rest secure with one set of assumptions. As fictional configurations of culture, they are lacking in single-minded moral purpose. Furthermore, they display skepticism for the role of culture in the formulation of human values. A society creates lies (*foma*, harmless truths, Bokonon calls them in *Cat's Cradle*) that feed the soul's hunger. Vonnegut is not so certain as Bokononists, however, of their harmlessness, for they often continue to warp the soul's bias past the time of their need. Is Christianity, he wonders, one of those *foma* which has lived beyond its effectuality, our punch-card technocracy having rendered it obsolete? "We would be a lot safer," Vonnegut told the graduating class of Bennington College in 1970, "if the Government would take its money out of science and put it into astrology and the reading of palms. I used to think that science would save us. But only in superstition is there hope. I beg you to believe in the most ridiculous superstition of all: that humanity is at the center of the universe, the fulfiller or the frustrater of the grandest dreams of God Almighty.

If you can believe that and make others believe it, human beings might stop treating each other like garbage."[11]

Behind this Barthian distrust of intrinsic ideas lurks an even more radical disdain for the climactic progression of human experience. "Nothing ever really ends," Vonnegut is reported to have remarked apropos of the ending of his play *Happy Birthday, Wanda June*. "Nothing in real life ends. 'Millicent at last understands.' Nobody ever understands."[12] This sentiment is shared by most Black Humorists. Their treatment of history differs from those writers in this century for whom progress is decay (such as T. S. Eliot or D. H. Lawrence or the Faulknerians); and from those for whom it is growth (such as Harold Robbins, Herman Wouk, Irving Stone, and the other latter-day Horatio Algerians). Nor does progress mean for them Giambattista Vico's cyclical concept of history, as it did for Joyce, who used it as a framework for his fiction. Closer to their view is that of the Tralfamadorians in Vonnegut's *The Sirens of Titan* and *Slaughterhouse-Five*, who see time as a vast memory bank, from which nothing is ever added or withdrawn. "It is just an illusion we have here on Earth," we are told in *Slaughterhouse-Five*, "that one moment follows another one, like beads on a string, and that once a moment is gone it is gone forever." Consequently, "When a Tralfamadorian sees a corpse, all he thinks is that the dead person is in bad condition in that particular moment, but that the same person is just fine in plenty of other moments" (p. 23). Understandably then, these novelists write out of a philosophical sense of the indeterminate as being the only reality available to man today—"that imminence of a revelation that is not yet produced" (to use Jorge Luis Borges' words), which is ultimately identifiable for these men—even interchangeable— with aesthetic reality.

The sense of imminent revelation is especially strong in Vonnegut's, Borges's, and Pynchon's fiction. For all three men it becomes a structural principle. Indeed, the patterns of *V.* offer little else than the apocalyptic conjurations of Herbert Stencil, who cheerfully admits that "no Situation had any objective reality: it only existed in the minds of those who happened to be in on it at any specific moment." And "Since these several minds tended to form a sum total or complex more mongrel than homogeneous, The Situation must necessarily appear to a single observer much like a diagram in four dimensions to an eye conditioned to seeing its world in only three" (ch. 7). Hence, Chapter 3 ("In which Stencil, a quick-change artist, does eight impersonations")—originally published as a short story "Under the Rose," acclaimed for its tight control, tragi-comic effect, and fusion of emotional depth and historical breadth[13]—was fractured by Pynchon into eight narrative points of view when he revised it for inclusion in *V.* The resultant "diffusion," which so upsets R. Sklar,[14] is a deliberate, controlled artifice for illustrating at the outset how Stencil—and the actors in the action—are forced to construct mirror theories to make comprehensible multi-form and simultaneous, rather than linear and sequential, events about which their knowledge is fragmentary and limited. It is either that or submit intellectually to the senseless drift and eddy of events. Like Smithson's "non-sites," *V.*'s reconstructed activities form a baroque parody of the human propensity to impose order, pattern, coherence, and meaning on unrelated events that seem to have something in common.

The difference between Pynchon's realizations and those of the previous three centuries, that reality is a construct of the human mind, is profound. Implicit in Pynchon's description of a situation as "more mongrel than homogeneous" when it exists in several minds is his reluctance to confirm any one observer as authoritative. Whereas a Blake, a Coleridge, or a John Stuart Mill could still believe in the intellectual systems of his own making, Pynchon (by way of Herbert Stencil) traces the successive configurations of V. into an historical conspiracy of baroque dimensions in time and space, conscious all the time that he is fabricating.

> As spread thighs are to the libertine, flights of migratory birds to the ornithologist, the working part of his tool bit to the production machinist, so was the letter V to young Stencil. He would dream perhaps once a week that it had all been a dream, and that now he'd awakened to discover the pursuit of V. was merely a scholarly quest after all, an adventure of the mind, in the tradition of *The Golden Bough* or *The White Goddess*. (ch. 3)

The crisis of faith in the evidence of one's senses is formulated in Pynchon's second novel *The Crying of Lot 49* with even greater insistence than in *V.* on the fundamental unreliability of the mind and with more powerful suggestion of the intangible mystery lurking on the edges of all our answers to the questions of daily existence. Confronted with overwhelming evidence that an underground communications system (W.A.S.T.E.), using Waste disposals among other means of distribution, has been in operation in America for more than a hundred years, Oedipa Maas stops short of conviction to wonder if she is romancing with fact, being hoaxed by an elaborate practical joke, or hallucinating:

> Either you have stumbled indeed, without the aid of LSD or other indole alkaloids, onto a secret richness and concealed density of dream; onto a network by which X number of Americans are truly communicating whilst reserving their lies, recitations of routine, arid betrayals of spiritual poverty, for the official government delivery system; maybe even onto a real alternative to the exitlessness, to the absence of surprise to life, that harrows the head of everybody American you know, and you too, sweetie. Or you are hallucinating it. Or a plot has been mounted against you, so expensive and elaborate, involving items like the forging of stamps and ancient books, constant surveillance of your movements, planting of post horn images all over San Francisco, bribing of librarians, hiring of professional actors and Pierce Inverarity only knows what-all besides, all financed out of the estate in a way either too secret or too involved for your non-legal mind to know about even though you are co-executor, so labyrinthine that it must have meaning beyond just a practical joke. Or you are fantasying some plot, in which case you are a nut, Oedipa, out of your skull. (ch. 6)

The thrust of the novel is toward convincing the reader, as well as Oedipa, of the possibility that there is "Another mode of meaning behind the obvious," that the ceaseless searching "among the dial's ten million possibilities for that magical Other" is not a hopelessly random exercise (ch. 6), that there is a meaningful pattern to seemingly pointless coincidences. Yet even as the narrative enacts this ploy, it confesses to a conclusiveness having only aesthetic validity. And at the finale, with the disclosure of what amounts to a fourth dimension where we would least suspect it, in our postal system, the narrative deliberately draws back from confirmation of its observations. Yet, even as it diffuses to include the possibility that Oedipa's conclusions may be the hallucinations of paranoia, it continues to formulate contrary premises in support of the existence of W.A.S.T.E.

In much Black Humor fiction there is a determined resistance of the narrative to confirm its own thesis. Assent is withheld from otherwise tenable and normative intellectual positions, including outright dissent. This programmatic skepticism has become one of the strategies used by Black Humorists for evoking a discursive world of not one but multiple unverifiable possibilities. In their willingness to resist the temptation to formulate answers, such authors as Vonnegut and Pynchon courageously rest with irresolveables. In this sense, *Cat's Cradle* and *God Bless You, Mr. Rosewater, V.* and *The Crying of Lot 49*, are honest novels.

NOTES TO CHAPTER III

1. See E. E. Bostetter, "The Nightmare World of *The Ancient Mariner*," *Studies in Romanticism*, I (1962), 241–254.

2. Cf. C. D. B. Bryan, "Kurt Vonnegut on Target," *New Republic*, LV (October 8, 1966), 21–22, 26; K. Allsop, *The Spectator*, No. 7166 (October 29, 1965), 554; [anon.], "Books Briefly Noted," *The New Yorker*, XLI (May 15, 1965), 216; Anne Duchene, *Manchester Guardian*, XCIII (November 25, 1965), 11; Eliot Fremont-Smith, *New York Times*, CXIV (April 9, 1965), L31; Martin Levin, "Do Human Beings Matter," *New York Times Book Review*, LXXVI (April 25, 1965), 41; Melvin Maddocks, *Christian Science Monitor*, LVII (May 6, 1965), B9; Judith Merrill, "Books," *Magazine of Fantasy and Science Fiction*, XXVII (1965), 78–83; [anon.], "Sweet and Sour Seventeen," *TLS* (November 11, 1965), p. 1007; Daniel Talbot, "Turning Bank Notes into Love Letters," *Sunday Herald Tribune: Book Week*, II (April 11, 1965), 6, 11; and [anon.], *Time*, LXXXV (May 7, 1965), 113–114.

3. "Give not that which is holy unto the dogs, neither cast ye your pearls before swine, lest they trample them under their feet and turn again and rend you" (*Matthew* 7:6).

4. I am paraphrasing here sentiments of Vonnegut speaking as narrator in *Slaughterhouse-Five* (p. 87).

5. Maxine Greene, "Aesthetics, Criticism, and the Work of Literary Art," *College English*, XXX (1968), 60. In my paraphrase of Steiner, I have followed Maxine Greene's comments.

6. Andrew Forge, "de Kooning in Retrospect," *ArtNews*, LXVIII (March, 1969), 61.

7. John Perreault, "The New de Koonings," *ArtNews*, LXVIII (March, 1969), 48.

8. Anthony Robbin, "Smithson's Non-site Sights," *ArtNews*, LXVII (February, 1969), 50.

9. "Floating Wit," *Time* (January 3, 1969), p. 44.

10. Frederick J. Hoffman, "Pynchon, Thomas 1937," *Contemporary Authors*, eds., James Ethridge, Barbara Kopal, and Carolyn Riley (Detroit, Michigan, 1963), XIX–XX, 353.

11. *Time* (June 29, 1970), p. 8.

12. *New York Times* (October 6, 1970), p. 56.

13. Robert Sklar, "The New Novel, USA: Thomas Pynchon," *The Nation*, CCV (September 25, 1967), 278.

14. *Ibid.*

65

IV

THE POLITICS OF PARODY; AND, THE COMIC APOCALYPSES OF JORGE LUIS BORGES, THOMAS BERGER, THOMAS PYNCHON, AND ROBERT COOVER

I

"I must create a system," Blake wrote, "or be enslaved by another's."[1] In the long history of western civilization man has created many value systems out of his urgency to explain the human situation. They generally fit in one form or another under the rubrics of philosophy, theology, science, or history. Much of the best Black Humor fiction parodies these frames of reference—these categorical imperatives—by means of which we organize the chaos of experience. Black Humor, however, in its representation of our various intrinsic value systems casts doubt on their objectivity and absoluteness even as it pays tribute to their ordered beauty.

Parody has traditionally provided its user with form and frame of reference, lending the weight of authority and convention to his strictures and exhortations. One thinks of Pope's Horatian odes and Johnson's Juvenalian reflections. Even with the mock epic, there is no question of the epic's position as a standard of value. A new skepticism, however, attends the parodic thrusts of Byron's *Don Juan*, that peculiarly modern poem, and of Joyce's *Ulysses*. While the older form is still accorded the respect of imitation, it is now also the target of the author's sallies of wit. In these works belief in traditional western values has not yet deteriorated to the point of outright rejection. Byron still clings to his belief in the damnation of sin, Joyce to his faith in the salvation of art. In the eyes of both, however, man is deheroicized; and the old conventions of form, which are implicit assertions of value, are treated irreverently. With the Black Humorists, even this limited assent to the traditional arrangements of human experience has become impossible.

To put it another way, one can define the symbiosis of man and nature as understood by the Romantics, say Coleridge, to consist of an intact physical world from which man has psychologically as well as theologically been separated. In this disjunction, art through its symbolic action is conceived of as the grand reconciler, uniting man once again with nature, and the artist is consequently applauded for his engagement with life. By the end of the nineteenth century, though, nature has become for the symbolists part of the primal fall, fragmented like human experience, no less ugly than evil. Now art serves the function of ordering and beautifying nature, and the artist necessarily is bent on disengaging himself and the work of art from the contingencies of life.[2] For the Black Humorist a teleological view of nature is no longer tenable. And with the departure of that faith goes the notion of art as a vehicle for resolving, reconciling, ordering, beautifying, or correcting nature. Art becomes indistinguishable from the other forms of nature, simply another "found" or equivalent object of life—succinctly epitomized by Borges's recognition, in his parable "A Yellow Rose," that "the tall, proud volumes casting a golden shadow in a corner were not—as his vanity had dreamed—a mirror of the world, but rather one thing more added to the world." In a world of endless equivalents, or alternatives, parody appears as a normative version of things.

Although his philosophical orientation is otherwise, G. D. Kiremidjian implicitly acknowledges as much in his essay on "The Aesthetics of Parody."[3] Kiremidjian's description of the relationship of art to the real world is that of the Realist. When the viable forms, intellectually and aesthetically, of a tradition can no longer succeed each other in time, historically, when in short the conventional forms are exhausted, he argues, then parody, especially self-parody, becomes an instrument in the hands of artists for re-establishing contact with the external world from which art has regularly derived its subject matter or content. But the existential Nominalism of this century has infiltrated his thinking in his definition of how parody effects this renewal of contact with the world of reality. "When art imitates itself, it in effect opposes another mirror to itself in parallel plane . . . and thus comes to embody the infinite possibility of natural phenomena. This process is not really an aesthetic intro-version but actually a kind of extroversion, in which the work breaks through its own artificial world, breaks through its own limitations, renounces in effect its own premises, and establishes an explicit literal relation with the real world beyond itself."[4]

Nabokov would agree with this statement, if the "real world" alluded to here is recognized to be no less artificial, no less a hall of mirrors, no less a continuum of refractions, than the aesthetic world of the novel. As he demonstrates at great length in *Lolita*, Humbert's error, not dissimilar to Kiremidjian's, merely its obverse, is his mistaking Lolita for his idealization of the nymphet, his identifying a mirrored reflection of his thoughts with a flesh-and-blood teeny-bopper. Black Humor insists that there is ultimately no reality we can possess other than the "glimmer lakes" of our fantasy; but we must recognize them as such. And therein lies Humbert's "sin" against existential reality. In Lolita, he confused for a few years the absolute with the temporal, and the abstract with the actual, a mistake he had not made in his previous visual "contacts" with nymphets nor in his initial Sunday morning solipsized seduction of Lolita. It is only in the "case history," in his aesthetic restructuring of the experience, that his passion acquires a reality not tragic, becomes a parody equivalent to the world. Contrariwise, Van Veen's "salvation" (in *Ada*) lies in his sophisticated apprehension of time as wholly personal and in his blithe disregard of space-time limitations in his narration (or refashioning) of the story of his and Ada's love.

The best Black Humor parodies offer us constructs of thought dazzlingly attractive in their aesthetic and intellectual coherence. We are asked to accept them as alternative formulations of values and systems, as a way of reminding us that they all—the fictionally conceived and the culturally received alike—are products of the human need to give pattern and order to experience and that they enjoy no independent existence apart from the one we bestow on them.

II

The witty *ficciones* of Borges are near perfect configurations of the mythic process, ordered forms that paradoxically confirm the infinite multiplication, the labyrinthine nightmare, of the world. Born like Nabokov into a society of flux and instability, caught between the cultures of Europe and Argentina, persecuted by Peron and rejected by his compatriots for not writing local color tales about gauchos, Borges has preferred the aesthetic labyrinths of his own making, with their parodic wink at the chaotic Great Labyrinth of the cosmos, to the absolutes of both western and eastern civilizations, with their humorless premises of rectitude and certitude.

In "Tlön, Uqbar, Orbis Tertius" he imagines a world posited on a set of categorical imperatives other than our own, or at least with a different orientation, a world whose language, religion, letters, and metaphysics presuppose idealism rather than materialism, in which the spatial does not persist in time but is replaced by time, the universe conceived as "a heterogeneous series of independent acts" rather than "a concourse of objects in space," as successive and temporal rather than spatial. Then, he conjectures what might happen if the evidential order of this fictional world, the creation of a secret and benevolent society begun in the seventeenth century, and numbering George Berkeley among its members, were to surface in the twentieth century and quickly supersede the old realities and their historical past. In this story a taut surface clarity masks a profound sense of the nightmarish choices available to the individual, and of the roles that chance and necessity play in this choice. The apocalyptic alteration in reality imagined here remains comic, however, because the mythic harmonies of the story never pretend to be other than invented, even though by means of this candor the story also reminds us of the human penchant to forget the intellectual origin of its myths. Once that fact is noted, the substitution of one myth for another can never be sinister, can never be other than comic.

Borges continually inveighs against the fatal tendency of man to mistake "symmetry with a semblance of order" for reality. Both "The Garden of Forking Paths" and "Death and the Compass" are dramatizations of this flaw in our mental life. The garden of Ts'ui Pên, "an incomplete, but not false, image of the universe," exists in time, not space, as "an infinite series of times, in a growing, dizzying net of divergent, convergent and parallel times." Yu Tsun, a grandson of Ts'ui Pên, operating in England as a spy for the German Imperial Army during World War I, erroneously interprets a series of coincidences, on the analogy with his ancestor's garden, as premonition that he is fated to murder the Sinologist Stephen Albert. The story ironically indicates that not one but many alternative actions, or forks in the garden, were available to Yu Tsun. The outer frame of the story further casts doubt on the validity of Yu Tsun's version of events. The murder of Dr. Albert was intended as a sign to the German command of a concentration of British artillery preparatory to an attack along the Serre-Montauban line. The opening paragraph of the story paraphrases Liddell Hart's *History of World War I*, in which torrential rains, not the bombing of the site consequent upon Yu Tsun's "message," caused a delay of five days in mounting the attack. Which is the real version of how and why the attack was postponed, the story asks: the subjective explanation of Yu Tsun or the objective explanation of Liddell Hart?

In "Death and the Compass," the detective Lönnrot scornfully rejects the suggestion of the police that "imaginary mischances of an imaginary robber" may explain the assassination of a delegate to the Third Talmudic Congress. He seeks rather "a purely rabbinical explanation." With irreproachable logic, he uses clues capable of cabalistic inferences to fit that and two subsequent killings into a Tetragrammaton of time and space which allows him to foretell the date and place of the next and final murder. His brilliant deduction leads him to his own death, for he is selected by his arch enemy the criminal Red Scharlach to be the fourth victim. The mystery whose symmetry and symbolism the master detective is bent on deciphering, that is, on discovering to have a meaningful order apprehensible by the mind, turns out to be a false, or made, "mystery" manipulated by the master criminal, who took advantage of the initial unintended killing to trap the relentlessly logical detective. Lönnrot's is the predicament of the human intellect committed to encoding the enigmatic and elusive contingencies of the universe. His rationality compels him to construct a labyrinth of events which he must then use, as if it were ineluctable reality, as a model for his actions.

Borges's radical skepticism will not allow the possibility of anything remaining fixed and certain. The only absolute he will entertain is that of flux and incertitude. "The Immortal" and "Pierre Menard, Author of the *Quixote*" are highly inventive, if disturbing parodies of this world picture. The fate of Homer, the archetype of the immortal poet, is rendered as one of changing conflations and of successive symbolic meanings, whose existence finally comprises only the separate instances of this tradition. In the long history of the Homeric tradition the poet who invented a tale about Ulysses becomes identified with the figure of the Wandering Jew (who surfaces in the story in 1929 as Cartaphilus, a Smyrnan antique dealer in quarto volumes of Pope's *Iliad*), with other nameless rhapsodists of folk literature, with adventurers, such as Sinbad, with Ulysses himself, and with successive soldiers down through history. Thus Homer literally vanishes into his tradition. "It is not strange that time should have confused the words that once represented me," Cartaphilus the Smyrnan dealer laments, "with those that were symbols of the fate of he who accompanied me for so many centuries. I have been Homer; shortly, I shall be No One, like Ulysses; shortly, I shall be all men; I shall be dead." The world contemplated here is profoundly impermanent. Neither archetypes nor words, the means by which a people link the present with the past, guarantees continuity and stability. "When the end draws near," Cartaphilus writes, "there no longer remain any remembered images; only words remain." And words are blank counters, resonant with different meanings at different times, meanings not necessarily cumulative. This is the point Pierre Menard makes with his recomposition of several chapters of *Don Quixote*. Verbally identical with Cervantes' novel, Menard's text turns out to mean something quite different, for the words and context of the seventeenth-century Spaniard convey a stylistic tone and a cultural attitude other than that of the twentieth-century French symbolist. In his duplication of *Don*

71

Quixote, Menard has simply added one more variant of experience to the long row of books already directed to that same goal.

Borges's stories are formally beautiful. Their aesthetic and philosophical symmetries are testaments to man's capacity to imagine order where only "divine disorder" obtains. And their strategies encompass both exigencies. As in "The Library of Babel"—where the library functions as a brilliant metaphor for the way fundamental laws descriptive of the universe are derived from visible but limited and fragmentary, ultimately irrational, evidence—they are superb parodies of the ordering intellect, while unequivocally confirmatory of the basic chaos of the cosmos.

III

The witty "fictions" of Borges have provided the younger Black Humorists with perfectly realized self-depreciatory, self-destructive models. This is not to say that they are merely attenuated mimics of Borges, although even if judged solely by their parodic intentions this possibility would not necessarily lend itself to a derogatory evaluation. Actually such American writers as Thomas Berger, Thomas Pynchon, Robert Coover, and John Barth, and such German and Canadian writers as Günter Grass and Leonard Cohen have been commendably inventive in adapting their parodies to the native materials of their respective national experiences and cultural destinies.

Little in Berger's previous novels—*Crazy in Berlin* and *Reinhart in Love*—prepares one for the epical sweep of *Little Big Man*, unless it is an unfocused thrust toward creation of myth in the Reinhart stories, or saga, with whom the first two novels and the most recent, *Vital Parts*, are concerned. *Little Big Man* is surely illustrative of how endemic the legend of the west is to the American imagination. To it must be ascribed the unexpected release of Berger's creative energies. In its comprehensive treatment of the west, the novel parodies the tall tale, both the Cooperian and the Twainian versions of the frontier, the concepts of the Indian as child of nature and as rapacious savage, the American dream of the virgin wilderness, and the Hollywood version of How the West Was Won. In time it spans the momentous decades from 1852 to

1876, when the Great Plains were wrested from the Indians, climaxing with the Battle of the Little Bighorn, America's most renowned military defeat, which paradoxically marked the end of the Indian menace. Here is apocalypse of such ironic ambiguity as to defeat any tragic impulse sought in the occasion.

The marvelous quality about the novel is that it does not rest content in being just another lampoon of the west. It begins that way, with considerable debunking of Indian, white settler, and U. S. Cavalry. The novel opens with Old Lodge Skins and his band of rag-tag, renegade Cheyenne drunkenly massacring the wagon train of Jack Crabb's family. Served whiskey instead of coffee, Old Lodge Skins and his fellow redskins react with buffoonery, childlike in their murderous frenzy and hangdog in the sobering light of the next day at the mayhem they have wrought not only on the whites but on each other as well. Yet out of this unpromising beginning emerges a novel of great power. By the end Old Lodge Skins has grown in heroic stature and in mythic dimensions much as does Natty Bumpo in the Leatherstocking tales.[5] More significantly, Jack Crabb comes dressed in the trappings of legend, the last in a long line of "sole survivors" to step forward with their eye-witness accounts of Custer's Last Stand. As a super western hero, Brian W. Dippie remarks, Crabb "is not so much exploding the old legends as . . . 'creating a new legend.' "[6] Crabb's boast that he was in on everything that happened in the west has true epical claims as the ultimate western boast, since as the "sole survivor" at age 111 of the Little Big Horn, he stands alone in undisputed command of the field; and his legend becomes part of the western myth, indeed displaces much of the existent lore. With Crabb at its center, the novel manages the near impossible feat of creating a new mythic synthesis of the major occurrences on the Plains in the third quarter of the nineteenth century—the massacre at the Washita, the construction of the transcontinental railroad, the trading along the Santa Fe Trail, the silver strike in the Rocky Mountains, the boom growth of Denver, the killing of the buffalo, and the hunting down of the Indians—and a reinterpretation of the characters of Hickok, Earp, Calamity Jane, and Custer, so convincing that no one reading the novel will be able again to assent easily to the previous legends, except as they and Berger's coincide.

Tone plays an important role in establishing this plausibility. Crabb's is the ingratiating manner of the down-to-earth unlettered chronicler, whose eye is concentrated on telling it as it was. He will not allow us to have any illusions about his prowess as a western hero. To enhance his height of five feet four inches, he wore built-up boots and a high-crowned Mexican sombrero. "In outline I was six foot tall," he tells us laconically, "but quite a bit of that was air" (ch. 12). The self-mockery here reaches beyond its immediate reference to deflate all the claims of the old legends of the west about men bigger than life. Wild Bill Hickok undergoes this reduction in reputation as gunfighter, preparatory to his reconstitution as a perfectionist in the handling of arms, a technician and an idealist. The first information Crabb learns about Hickok is that "he took care of the McCanles gang ten year ago at the Rock Crick stage station down in Jefferson County. There was six of them . . . and they come for Wild Bill, and he took three with his pistols, two with his bowie, and just beat the other to death with a gunstock." Crabb's reaction is to reduce "that by half in my mind." "I had been on the frontier from the age of ten on," he reminds us, "and knew a thing as to how fights are conducted. When you run into a story of more than three against one and one winning, then you have heard a lie. I found out later I was right in this case: Wild Bill killed only McCanles and two of his partners, and all from ambush" (ch. 20). Thus, Crabb's candor performs two functions. It deflates the exaggerated claims of the old west; and it also prepares us to accept the new mythicizing process that the novel is imposing on these western materials. By means of the former, the act of essential honesty of tone—and hence of contents—is constantly reaffirmed, making creditable the ensuing renewal of the myth in the latter act.

A further factor in Berger's bringing off this literary achievement lies in his selection of the right time in the history of the winning of the west and of the right climactic episode—Custer's Last Stand—which ambiguously marked both an ending and a beginning, a defeat and a victory, an apocalypse and a millenium. Of equal importance for the success of the parody is that Berger treats his sources—"60 or 70 accounts of the Western reality" were read as preparation for writing the novel—"[7] with respect. The facts are not distorted for fictional purposes. Old Lodge Skins' death derives almost verbatim from John G. Neihardt's account of *Black Elk . . . the Life Story of a Holy Man of the Oglala Sioux* (1932). Custer's mad talk at his Last Stand is lifted from his account of *My Life on the Plains*. Details of Indian life, of Hickok's gun skill, of buffalo killing, and the myriad other details of Plains life in the fifties, sixties, and seventies are integral to the mythic superstructure. Jack Crabb—wholly fictional—merges with both history and legend in the parallels of his conception with a Jack Cleybourne who allegedly was captured by Cheyennes in 1866 and witnessed the Massacre at Washita in 1868, and with a John Clayton who is portrayed in Will Henry's novel *No Survivors* as a southern Confederate officer living with the Sioux and present at the Battle of Little Big Horn.[8] Such care for history protects the novel from being mistaken for a mere hoax.

Although its adroit blend of fact and fiction wins our acceptance as a plausible ordering of western experience, *Little Big Man* in its very form as novel calls our attention to the fictive processes of legend. In this respect it is a parody of the western myth very much in the mode of Borges's *ficciones*, but reflective of what is indigenous to America, the homespun wisdom and the frontier psychology, the peculiar sprawl and untidiness of the American ethos. Delight in the contraries of shrewdness and gullibility has characterized the American from Ben Franklin to Twain and Faulkner. Berger finds its appeal especially seductive. The outer frame of the Foreword and Editor's Epilogue is by one Ralph Fielding Snell, "Man of Letters," whose pedantic and conventional response to the materials of Crabb's life lends inadvertent authenticity to the rascally but ingratiating claims of Crabb. Snell's remarks remind us of the equally obtuse Foreword of John Ray, Jr., Ph.D. in *Lolita*. The device in both novels is the author's way, in part, of informing us that he is in control.

Despite its faint aura of archaism, *Little Big Man*, like Borges's stories and Nabokov's *Lolita* and *Ada*, is unmistakably a novel of the sixties, preoccupied with the clash of cultures and of life styles. Jack Crabb is a man caught between two worlds, uncommitted wholly to either, and the narrative pattern of his oscillation between Indian and white societies illustrates this fact. Delbert E. Wylder is probably right to insist that the foibles of both whites and Indians

75

are seen from the perspective of the opposite culture, and hence the novel is a "commentary on the foibles of mankind rather than a simplified statement about the superiority of Indian ways."[9] Yet this intuition risks being simplistic, too easily overlooking the special definition of the Indian's vision of life as a "Sacred Hoop" or mystical circle, and the special application of this philosophy to a growing subculture in America. When Jack Crabb accompanies Old Lodge Skins to the summit of one of the Bighorn Mountains, where the aged Indian prepares to die, he looks up at the sky and remarks:

> I don't think I ever seen a sky as big as that one, or as clear. Real pale blue it was, like a dome made of sapphire, except to say that makes you think it was enclosed, but it wasn't: it was open and unlimited. If you was a bird you could keep going straight up forever, fast as you could fly, yet you would always be in the same place.
>
> Looking at the great universal circle, my dizziness grew still, I wasn't wobbling no more. I was there, in movement, yet at the center of the world, where all is self-explanatory merely because it *is*. Being at the Greasy Grass or not, and on whichever side, and having survived or perished, never made no difference.
>
> We had all been men. Up there, on the mountain, there was no separations. (ch. 30)

Here is the Cheyenne philosophy of life encapsulated in the novel. Rather than disjunction between man and nature, a mystical unity persists, in which man finds himself always at the center of his world. There is no circumference to bind him in. As Blake puts it in *Jerusalem* (plate 71, lines 6–8): "What is Above is Within, for every-thing in Eternity is translucent:/ The Circumference is Within," and is always expanding "forward to Eternity." If man "move his dwelling-place, his heavens also move/ Where'er he goes" (*Milton*, plate 29, lines 12–13). Hence there is not one version of reality but many. Each Indian contains his own world; he is "a man who must do what is in his heart and no one can question it" (ch. 7). He does not follow a leader but rather chooses to go in the same direction or to the same place as another. Contrariwise, the white submits to authority to realize aims external to his immediate personal needs. The men of the Seventh Cavalry bicker among themselves and hate some of their officers; but they work and fight as a disciplined unit. The philosophy of life of the Indian is identity conscious, while that of the white man is goal-oriented. This contrast of life styles characterizes today's division between the under thirty and the over thirty, between a version of reality concentrating on what one is and a version extolling what one does. It is not accidental then that the sixties have witnessed an extraordinary idealization of Indian ways among young Americans. Nor is it difficult to understand the enthusiastic reception accorded *Little Big Man* by both academics (as Black Humor) and populace (as western legend).

IV

A more inclusive purchase on history is taken by Thomas Pynchon's baroque first novel *V.*, which parodies the compulsion of the human mind to find pattern in events—and to create a pattern where none manifests itself. On the literary level, the novel strives to be omnibus: to ape the spy tale, the romance, the political novel, the Oedipus quest, and the documentary; to echo the symbolic texture of Conrad, the complex dreams of Freud, the social commentary of Dos Passos, the technocratic apprehension of science fiction, the aesthetic decadence of Nabokov, the vapid heroics of comic opera and of Victorian adventure stories, the wasteland mythography of Eliot, the *Sehnsucht* utopianism of *Lost Horizon*, the moral vision of Faulkner, and even the acrid iconoclasm of Black Humor. If its parody of literature is not absolute, its ambition is surely in that direction. But it is on history that the novel concentrates its central statement, which is portrayed as possibly man's most foolish exercise in shaping experience into meaning, because the result diverges so patently from the truth. Opposed to history as conventionally conceived and formulated, *V.* presents a world kaleidoscopically complicated and ultimately inimical to assigned significance. The mythical political entity of Vheissu, that asiatic-antarctic Shangri-la of old Godolphin, a "country of coincidence, ruled by a ministry of myth," is a fully realized correlative of the world of *V.* A pun on *Wie heisst du* (what is your name?), it is empty of meaning, its history of linked persons and places adding

77

up "only to the recurrence of an initial and a few dead objects" (ch. 16), as Herbert Stencil reluctantly admits to himself in Malta at the end of the spoor he has followed across continents of space and half a century of time. Its blankness, its unidentifiability—because so protean—is similarly attested to by old Godolphin when he describes Vheissu to Victoria Wren as totally inconstant: "Everything changes. The mountains, the lowlands are never the same color from one hour to the next. No sequence of colors is the same from day to day" (ch. 7). In this respect, Pynchon, like Barth, equates multiplicity—the horrifying flux of life—with the void.

In a narrower historical sense, however, the novel takes for its paradigm of nothingness the Dulles-Eisenhower years of brinksmanship—Communist Conspiracy, Cold War, Domino Theory, and Atom Bomb Threat. The ghost of annihilation haunts each of the Stencil-V. episodes of the novel. As Robert Sklar has noted, disapprovingly,[10] the word *apocalypse* reverberates through its pages. He might also have mentioned the word *holocaust*, which appears with no less frequency. Both words underscore the war neurosis of the fifties, when it was believed, in the words of Stencil, that "Events seem to be ordered into an ominous logic" (ch. 16). Stencil's vision of history as a "grand cabal" (ch. 7) is Dulles' and the State Department's. It is a version of events perfectly realized in Stencil's recreation of the "Venezuelan problem" in Florence in April, 1899. Confronted with a romantic Gaucho bent on working a Venezuelan rebellion, a larcenous Italian plotting to steal the Botticelli *Birth of Venus* from the Uffizi, and an addled English naval captain fleeing the chimeras of his years in foreign climes—all coincidentally meeting in Florence—Stencil imagines the Foreign Office Section of the British Consulate fearfully trying to unravel what Stencil *père* is made to call "this abstract entity The Situation, its idea, the details of its mechanism." Young Godolphin expresses the concern of everyone when he comments: "Their anxiety is the same as my father's, what is coming to be my own, and perhaps in a few weeks what will be the anxiety of everyone living in a world none of us wants to see lit into holocaust." And all this *Angst* originates in "a Situation which refused to make sense no matter who looked at it, or from what angle" (ch. 7)! A situation which we learn from the narrative is nonexistent. Yet it becomes its own *raison d'être*, a means of ordering events into a context of reality, and in that way acquiring actuality.

Pynchon parodies the paranoic bravura of the state department, its proclivity for finding patterns of conspiracy in unrelated incidents, conspiracies which displace the actual event and determine future responses to new occurrences. The abstractness of the perennial Situation, its undesignated and unindividualized nature, recurs in the variety of references to it: Nameless Horror, Things in the Back Room, June Disturbances, The Situation as an N-Dash, the Ultimate Plot Which Has No Name. The metamorphoses of V. as *femme fatale*—Victoria Wren (Cairo and Florence, 1899), mysterious lady (Paris, 1913), Veronica Manganese (Valletta, 1919), Vera Monroving (Warmbad, South West Africa, 1922), and the Bad Priest (Valletta, 1940)—become successive objective correlatives of the state department theory of the persistence of the threat to political order and stability. That V. is always present at places of revolution or insurrection—albeit of minor or even irrelevant importance—satirizes the state department's predilection for seeing a continuity of plot, worldwide in dimension, where no such cabal may exist, and for following a policy of reacting only at times of imagined crisis. The possibility that no causality connects one happening to another or to a central subversive plan is slyly suggested by the different identities of V., as also by the nonchronological narration of the Stencil-V. episodes: Cairo (1899), Florence (1899), Warmbad (1922), Valletta (1940), Paris (1913), Valletta (1919). There is additionally the confusion of historical fact with fictional invention. The novel purports to be a record of verifiable political incidents; but the factual is so skillfully joined with the fanciful that one is unable offhand to tell them apart. We are disconcertingly conscious that the author is engaged in a colossal put-on. Consequently, we uneasily withhold our assent to even the purely historical allusions, the Fashoda affair with Kitchener in Egypt, the colonial policy of Germany in South West Africa, the self-rule aspirations of the Maltese after the First World War.

The world of *V.* is pluralistic, one of unlimited points of view, with reality presumably emergent out of the reconciliation of these diverse perceptions. Thus chancelleries all over the world piece together their picture of an ever-threatening but unknown enemy.

79

And thus both the Stencils—father and son, British Foreign Office agent and amateur historian in search of his past—grope to connect their scraps of information into a coherent design, Stencil *père* on the scene, so to speak, at first hand and Stencil *fils* at second hand from the tantalizing *memento mori* of his father. This patchwork quilt approach to reality is brilliantly dramatized by Pynchon in the eight versions of the narrative action (more accurately the eight points of view imagined by Herbert Stencil) that comprise all we learn of the intrigues of British spies in Egypt on the eve of the Fashoda incident. The irony is that the eye witnesses are all peripheral to the action. From the casual observation and incidental eavesdropping of a cafe waiter, a hotel factotum, an English confidence man (who is incidentally a blatant parody of Humbert Humbert), a train conductor, a garry driver, a burglar, and a beer-hall waitress, only a fragmentary conception of what is happening can be constructed. It is as if the Fashoda incident were rendered on seven picture postcards and mailed by foreign correspondents unable to find transportation to the front or wire service to the home office. Nor in the culmination of the action are we helped to any understanding of what the spies were about. Narrated omnisciently in the elliptical manner of stage directions for a melodrama, the situation is left, as Sklar has complained, "deliberately shrouded in mystery."[11] But is not that Pynchon's point about what men call history? that it is an omnia gathering of irrelevancies from which sense is manufactured.

The same procedure directs the conception of the Stencil-V. episodes. Each is a parody of a different frame of reference by which our knowledge of experience is recorded: as uninvolved eye witness (Egypt, chapter 3), as inadvertent participant (Florence, chapter 7), as personal remembrance (South West Africa, chapter 9) as journal record (Malta, chapter 11), and as contriver of events (Malta, Epilogue). Obviously, none is the whole truth. Nor does the novel offer to combine them into a full explanation, its point being that such truth is impossible to know. We are left with incomplete versions of experience, which the mode of presentation, as Stencil's formulations mostly twice removed from the original action, is meant ironically to suggest.

The refusal of the novel to reconcile its voices is also, however, a method of transforming potential holocaust into comic apocalypse. The two principal narrative voices are those of Herbert Stencil and of Benny Profane. Both reflect the entropic man-machine thesis developed in the novel. As such both are parodies of twentieth-century man, the profaned and stenciled products of a state department, scientific-political, industrial-military complex. The movements of both form parabolas of motion admirably summarized by the yo-yo image. Stencil's is larger in time and space than Profane's, incorporating his father's apogee in Malta in 1919 to his own apodosis in Malta in 1956. But the application of dehumanizing force is the same. The pertinence of the Second Law of Thermodynamics to the man-machine thesis and to the obsession of V. for incorporating inert matter into her body has been commented on by more than one critic.[12] Nor is it difficult to find a correspondence between the notion of entropy and the state department neurosis that order and stability are forever threatening to deteriorate into disorder and chaos. On that basis, the Stencil sections may be linked thematically to the Profane plot.

Still, the two lines of narrative development, like the dual plots of an Elizabethan play, are more often in polarity to each other than in fusion, Profane's peregrinations only inadvertently and at intervals entering the gravitational field of Stencil's temporal and spatial ellipsis. In essentials the two are antithetical, Stencil a quest hero, Profane an anti-hero. Despite his recognition of the quixotic nature of his pursuit of V., Stencil persists in the quest even after he has tracked V. to her death, spinning off at the end of the novel to follow new trails leading him hopefully to the disassembled and scattered pieces of inert matter that once were parts of her body. Thus begins the third (but unnarrated) stage of the comedy of V., if we count the father's contretemps with her and the son's reconstruction of them the first and the second, each clearly marking successive phases of entropy. Profane, abandoned by Stencil in Malta, is last seen dressed in levis, suede jacket, and cowboy hat, running down a street of Valletta, hand in hand with a girl, in a repetition of his action in Norfolk nine months earlier, when he was introduced to us in Chapter 1. He is still mindlessly yo-yoing.

In the refusal of the narrative to reconcile the Profane-Stencil plots, V. denies its own clangorous assertions about the imminence of holocaust in favor of a comic (that is, uncompleted) apocalypse, even while, ironically, using as a setting for the final Malta scenes the Suez Canal crisis of 1956. In the formulation of its myth of apocalypse, the novel perversely includes a refutation of that myth. If it presents history as an endless series of impending catastrophes, of giant cabals bent on creation of riot, and as a paranoic struggle of established (and good) powers with mysterious evil forces, its elaborate configurations also present paradigmatically the view that history is ultimately unapprehensible,[13] merely various limited, impercipient moments of consciousness and contact. As confirmation of this aperçu, *V.* never adds up to one unified statement. It cheerfully remains a congeries of "histories" of the lady V.: the British Foreign Office's official version; Herbert Stencil's reconstructions of Mondaugen's and Porcepic's stories, of young Godolphin's odyssey, and above all of his father's professional life; Profane's voyeuristic yo-yoings; Fausto Maijstral's and Father Fairing's journal accounts —diverse and incomplete versions of what possibly happened. None has precedence of truth over the others and none confirms the threat of disorder that each separately presumes in the story of V.'s diaspora to be the harbinger of.

V

Borges tells a story ("The Circular Ruins") of a magician who dreams a man into being with minute integrity and inserts him into reality, only to make the humiliating discovery after such strenuous effort that he is himself in turn a phantom, "a mere appearance, dreamt by another" more powerful demiurge. Robert Coover, like Borges, addresses himself to the ultimate questions of the cosmos, infinity, eternity, and First Cause. In his second novel *The Universal Baseball Association*, he uses the national pastime of baseball for the context of a similar representation of this world as the fantasied creation of a less than divine gamesman sitting at his kitchen table, playing a dice game and keeping records of the results.

The appeal of baseball is as much statistical as heroic, as much a ritual of numbers and record keeping as of manly encounters and athletic skills. The variety of data—fielding and hitting totals and averages from year to year for individual and for team—is endless.

The mystik of numbers surrounding baseball is summarized by J. Henry Waugh, sole proprietor (that is, inventor) of the Universal Baseball Association (UBA) and the dice game through which its history unfolds:

> Moreover, seven—the number of opponents each team now had—was central to baseball. Of course, nine, as the square of three, was also important: nine innings, nine players, three strikes each for three batters each inning, and so on, but even in the majors there were complaints about ten-team leagues, and back earlier in the century, when they'd tried to promote a nine-game World Series in place of the traditional best-out-of-seven, the idea had failed to catch on. Maybe it all went back to the days when games were decided, not by the best score in nine innings, but by the first team to score twenty-one runs . . . three times seven. Now there were seven fielders, three in the outfield and four in the infield, plus the isolate genius on the mound and the team playmaker and unifier behind the plate; seven pitches, three strikes and four balls; three basic activities—pitching, hitting, and fielding—performed around four bases. . . . In the UBA, each team played its seven opponents twelve times each, and though games lasted nine innings, they got turned on in the seventh with the ritual mid-inning stretch. (ch. 7)

It is this concentration on rules, averages, and figures, so extravagantly displayed at the Baseball Hall of Fame and Museum in Cooperstown, New York, that Coover asks us to accept as an objective correlative of the Biblical story of man and of the Judeo-Christian version of an orderly, meaningful cosmos.

To underscore his belief that such a world observes logically an illogical set of laws, Coover does not write actually about baseball but rather parodies it in the form of a dice game—the latest and most complex of many thought up by J. Henry Waugh (or JHWH, Yahweh, as the acronym of his name suggests), a disreputable accountant inclined to booze and B-girls, with a knack for figures, percentages, and records, a middle-aged bachelor filling his nights with something to do. Nor does Waugh use realistic props to bring the teams, the playing field, and crowds alive. He sits at his kitchen table, rolling his dice, surrounded by piles of paper slips, the score cards on each game. Thus, for all the pretence at order and pattern subsumed in the statistics, irrational chance and personal whim, not without its inference of solipsistic idealism, actually direct the results. As Waugh admits, "Even though he'd set his own rules, his own limits, and though he could change them whenever he wished, nevertheless he and his players were committed to the turns of the mindless and unpredictable—one might even say, irresponsible—dice." Yet, "when continuity and pattern dissipated, giving way to mere accident," he influenced the game in inexplicit and imprecise ways:

> Henry remembered how he himself had wearied finally of the Pioneer domination, and how, secretly, he had rooted for any and all challengers. Of course, he hadn't interfered directly in any way, and yet the Pioneers must have felt, somehow, his resistance, and in ways not really visible, he had probably in fact made it harder for them. (ch. 2)

And at least once, he intervenes directly, arranging the dice so that the pitcher Jock Casey is struck fatally by a line-drive.

Coover skillfully parallels the events of the UBA and its eight teams with those of the Old Testament. Crisis strikes in the fifty-sixth season (Waugh manages to play a full season of games and log the results every two months), when Pioneer rookie Damon Rutherford, who had pitched a perfect game several days earlier, is fatally beanballed by Knickerbocker rookie Jock Casey. With the close of that season, Waugh feels the need for some special commemoration to perk up his jaded interest in the game. He decides on "a compact league history, a book about these fifty-six years. Needn't be an official history, could even be a little controversial, the exposure of some pattern or other" (ch. 7). He catches inspiration from the idea and soon is elaborating on the significance of those seasons and conceiving of the book's authorship by one of the league's participants:

> It was all there in the volumes of the Book and in the records, but now it needed a new ordering, perspective, personal vision, the disclosure of pattern, because he'd discovered—who had discovered? Barney maybe—yes, Barney Bancroft had discovered that perfection wasn't a thing, a closed moment, a static fact, but *process*, yes, and the process was transformation, and so Casey had participated in the perfection, too, maybe more than anybody, for even Henry had been affected, and Barney was going to write it. (ch. 7)

Thus ends the penultimate chapter and the primary (old testamentary) narrative of the novel (and of man). In the eighth and final chapter, the history of the league is reckoned by a new calendar, beginning with the death of Damon Rutherford. It is now Damonsday CLVII. Henry Waugh is conspicuously absent from the narrative action. There is only a younger generation of players split into contrary sects and schisms, debating the meaning of the game whose rules they observe and whose apocalyptic events (mainly of Damonsday I) they annually re-enact.

In considerable detail not indicated by this brief summary, the novel parodies the Old and New Testament accounts of man, as well as such post-Christian theological controversies as "Of Providence, Foreknowledge, Will and Fate,/ Fixt Fate, free will, foreknowledge absolute,"[14] of transubstantiation and the reality of the communion host, evolutionary doctrine and the perfectibility of man, existential skepticism and the notion that God is dead. Similarly, it is apparent to baseball aficionados that the narrative parodies the history of baseball, especially the crucial innovations and developments pioneered by Alexander Joy Cartwright and Henry Chadwick. Reverently apotheosized at Cooperstown as the "Father of Modern Base Ball," Cartwright "set bases 90 feet apart [and] established 9 innings as game and 9 players as team." He also organized the Knickerbocker Baseball Club in 1845. Chadwick's contributions to the game, also memorialized at Cooperstown included "inventor of the box score, author of the first rule-book in 1858, [and] chairman of rules committee in the first nation-wide baseball organization." It is interesting to note that the seventh chapter marks not only the end of the old testamentary era (the first fifty-six seasons of the UBA) but also represents the seventh-inning stretch. The novel conspicuously lacks a ninth chapter (inning), because the new testamentary era of the league (that is, of the ballgame) is still being played.

To combine the two fables, one sacred, the other profane, as authored by a rummy bookkeeper, is to call into question the fabulous, or divine, explanation of the universe. Order, balance, pattern, and continuity become unavoidably suspect. So Knickerbocker rookie Hardy Ingram conjectures on Damonsday CLVII, preparatory to assuming the guise of Damon Rutherford for the annual

85

Parable of the Duel. Donning a jersey lettered with a "bold anti-quated 'I' " he wonders if the uniform transforms him into Damon:

> Probably not: too pat. Numerology. Lot of revealing work in that field lately. Made you wonder about a lot of things. Like the idea Damon was killed in Game 49: seven times seven. Third inning. Unbelievable. Or like that guy who's discovered that the whole damn structure from the inning or organization up and double entry bookkeeping are virtually identical: just multiply it by twenty-one, the guy claims, and you've got it all. Grim idea. (ch. 8)

The organization of the novel—seven chapters depicting the fifty-sixth season with its epochal deaths on separate occasions of Damon Rutherford and Jock Casey, and an eighth in which the two occurrences have been "squeezed . . . into one ceremony" and conflated with "the ancient myths of the sun, symbolized as a victim slaughtered by the monster or force of darkness" (leaving a ninth chapter —or inning—in the history of the world still to be played?)— allows us to witness parodically how man gives continuity and order to chaos, founds, in rookie Ingram's words, "old-fashioned humanism . . . on abiding ignorance and despair," and enacts "old rituals of resistance and rot" to body forth "the ontological revelations of the patterns of history" (ch. 8).

VI

Rookie Hardy Ingram's unconscious allusion to J. Henry Waugh, founder and sole proprietor of the Universal Baseball Association, Inc., when he conjectures about the double entry bookkeeping structure of baseball (that is, of life), reveals in Coover a sophistication with myth that compares favorably to earlier attempts in this mode, Malamud's *The Natural* for instance, another novel which tries to turn the legendary elements of baseball into serious fictional statement. The numerology of the game would seem to lend itself to the ritual schemata of Malamud, when in fact its pseudo air of regularity coincides more readily with the mythic skepticism of Coover. That Coover recognized this is a tribute to his literary acumen. Additionally, Coover like many other Black Humorists of his generation displays an inventiveness that the generation of Malamud, Bellow, and Mailer lacks. This skill appears in their concern for plot and sensitivity for correspondences to the absurd world. In their attention to plot, scene setting, and narrative pace, they are not unlike such contemporary British novelists as Kingsley Amis, John Osborne, John Braine, and Angus Wilson, who have bypassed the great novelists of the earlier part of this century—Conrad, Joyce, Woolf and their analyses of the deep structures of personality—for the social realism at the turn of the century of H. G. Wells, Arnold Bennett, and John Galsworthy.

One of the aesthetic pleasures of Black Humor derives from the parodic aptness of its fictional worlds, from the deftness with which these fictional microcosms mirror the profound disjunctions of contemporary life. Stanley Elkin's use of the arbitrary illogicalities of the modern penitentiary (inhabited by few true penitents) in *A Bad Man* is an unsubtle instance, partly because of its undigested Kafkan matter and *Catch-22* manner. But *The Sot-Weed Factor* is a brilliant parody of the eighteenth-century novel and world picture; and contrary to Earl Rovit's judgment the parody is not indulged in for its own sake. It is difficult to square the actualities of the novel with Rovit's assertion that Barth in "denying himself access to the speech of his own time" has written "that kind of imitation which is frozen into the inflexible forms of that which it is meant to ridicule."[15] The fact is that Barth does not maintain the mannered language of the opening pages at all times. Like a conductor who drills an orchestra on the opening movement of a symphony to a greater extent than on the middle passages, Barth relaxes his style repeatedly in later portions of the narrative, particularly restricting his balanced and antithetical language to the speeches of his characters. And the eighteenth-century speech of Ebenezer and Burlingame is obviously a pastiche that we are meant to recognize as such, for theirs are twentieth-century sensibilities responding to a modern world of "blind Nature [which] has neither codes nor causes" (III, 18). Unlike the *discordia concors* of the eighteenth-century novel, with its affirmation of order, *The Sot-Weed Factor* consistently confirms Burlingame's vision of the world and the soul of man as parts of "that same black Cosmos whence we sprang and through which we fall: the infinite wind of space" (II, 23). Burlingame envisions chaos, not order, as the lot of man; and the novel supports him. It gives us a comic version of the American dream. The early Puritan colonists sought out America as a new Eden where man could reverse the history of his fallen state. Ebenezer contrariwise brings his innocence to the New World where it is corrupted, where Indian savagery lacks nobility, and where the wilderness is less virginal paradise than a place in which pox infects the unwary, and chicanery and vice prevail, in which sex is not productive of life but of disintegration, and innocence is equated with ignorance. The final repudiation of the Great American Garden comes when Ebenezer and his sister sell the family plantation and move into town. Clearly the world explored in *The Sot-Weed Factor* partakes less of the social-contract idealism of Jeffersonian America, a community of farmers peopled with the chosen of God, than of the psychic and social realities of post-war America, its customs, institutions, and deepest ordinances of society, its cancerous productivity of faceless urban tracts like Los Angeles without center or purpose other than to provide bedrooms for its inhabitants, and its obsessive conformity to the norms of decaying institutions. Thus, Rovit misses the mark in his apprehension of the purpose of the parody in *The Sot-Weed Factor*, for the limitation Barth is getting at is experiential, not verbal and stylistic. In a world in which logical cause and effect is absent, the only way of arriving at the "truth" of experience is to know *all* the possible causes of an occurrence. Such exhaustion of the antecedents of experience cannot be reconciled with the limitations of being human. And the perspective of the eighteenth century with its historically inherited belief, albeit desperately strained, in a meaningful circumscribed cosmos ironically focuses our reception to the world of flux depicted in *The Sot-Weed Factor*.

For the Black Humorist, parody does not figure in its traditional form as a device (in the words of Earl Rovit's definition) for realizing final answers when "confronted with an unlimited choice among equally cogent values."[16] Rather it offers one more way of formulating unanswerable questions. In the Black Humorist's hands parody provides a means of giving form and perspective to the diversity of experience, of controlling and arranging it with sufficient artistry to embody a coherence that has internal logic if little necessary relationship to the outer coincidence of facts. Black Humor parody thus leaves unconfirmed the question of the reality of the events narrated. If the raw data of experience is beyond human apprehension unless categorized, and the traditional value categories are no longer viable, then man must invent his history, must consciously mythopoetize his experience. He may dismiss his life, like Burlingame, as cosmically irrelevant. He may immemorialize it, like Humbert Humbert and Van Veen, into an art form. He may nervously do both, like Oskar in *The Tin Drum*. Ideally, Black Humor parody is multiform, as in *Lolita*, *V.*, and *The Tin Drum*, for it is a version of metamorphosis protean in its capacity for equivalences. Such a fictional treatment of persons and places departs radically from the logic of cause and effect, the consanguinity of relationship, and the consecutiveness of history. It allows Oskar to be simultaneously the child of three and the man of thirty, able at one moment to drum his conscience into forgetfulness and at another to drum up recall of the past in an act of contrition. It allows Humbert to view all nymphets as instances of the archetypal nymphet, whether Annabel or Lolita or other pre-teen school girls. It allows him to re-invent his past endlessly, so long as he does not merge it with another's past or thrust it into another's world. It allows Jack Crabb to participate in all the legendary exploits of the west, and to embody as parts of his being like Blake's mythical Albion those of England the manifold features of the westerner. It allows Borges, Barth, Nabokov, Pynchon, Berger, Coover, Grass, and Cohen to invent pseudo-histories as "real" as the official histories, so long as they do not try to displace one version with another. It is a testimony to the honesty of these writers that they remain consistent to their view of the anonymity of person and the multiplicity of event, that they do not succumb to the temptation of the absolutist.

NOTES TO CHAPTER IV

1. *Jerusalem*, plate 10, line 20. The speaker is actually Los.
2. For a discussion of the historical evolution of the aims of art, see M. H. Abrams, "Coleridge, Baudelaire, and Modernist Poetics," *Immanente Aesthetik—Aesthetische Reflexion—Lyrik als Paradigma der Moderne*, ed. W. Iser (Munich, 1966), pp. 113–138.
3. *Journal of Aesthetics and Art*, XXVIII (1969), 231–242.

4. *Ibid.*, p. 238.

5. Delbert E. Wylder, "Thomas Berger's *Little Big Man* as Literature," *Western American Literature*, III (1969), 273–284.

6. "Jack Crabb and the Sole Survivors of Custer's Last Stand," *Western American Literature*, IV (1969), 201. Dippie is quoting Granville Hicks in part here.

7. Quoted by Jay Gurian, "Style in the Literary Desert: *Little Big Man*," *Western American Literature*, III (1969), 285–296.

8. Brian W. Dippie, "Jack Crabb and the Sole Survivors of Custer's Last Stand."

9. "Thomas Berger's *Little Big Man* as Literature," p. 283.

10. "The New Novel, U.S.A.: Thomas Pynchon," *The Nation*, CCV (September 25, 1967), 278.

11. *Ibid.*

12. See Don Hausdorff, "Thomas Pynchon's Multiple Absurdities," *Wisconsin Studies in Contemporary Literature*, VII (1966), 258–269.

13. Cf. James D. Young, "The Enigma Variations of Thomas Pynchon," *Critique*, X (1968), 69–77.

14. John Milton, *Paradise Lost*, II, 559–560.

15. "The Novel as Parody: John Barth," *Critique*, VI (1963), 82.

16. *Ibid.*, p. 80.

V

THE AESTHETICS OF ANXIETY; AND, THE CONFORMIST HEROES OF BRUCE JAY FRIEDMAN AND CHARLES WRIGHT

I

In his portrait of Colonel Cathcart in *Catch-22*, Joseph Heller defines the *Angst* of the small, aspiring, flattened, big, weak *Massenmensch* of our century. The Colonel is the nemesis of Yossarian, yet ironically shares with Yossarian the anxiety that afflicts man faced with his own helplessness and insignificance before the diffusion of twentieth-century mass society. Despite his being an eager student of the rules and taboos of the military, he is perpetually beset with uncertainty. He is

> a slick, successful, slipshod, unhappy man of thirty-six who lumbered when he walked and wanted to be a general. . . . He was complacent and insecure, daring in the administrative stratagems he employed to bring himself to the attention of his superiors and craven in his concern that his schemes might all backfire.

Not to know at any given moment the moods of his superiors and the situation at GHQ is the nightmare of his life. Hence he "was on the alert constantly for every signal, shrewdly sensitive to relationships and situations that did not exist. He was someone in the know who was always striving pathetically to find out what was going on.

He was a blustering, intrepid bully who brooded inconsolably over the terrible ineradicable impressions he knew he kept making on people of prominence who were scarcely aware that he was even alive." Colonel Cathcart lives "by his wits in an unstable, arithmetical world of black eyes and feathers in his cap, of overwhelming imaginary triumphs and catastrophic imaginary defeats" (ch. 19).

Here is no Byronic superhero, no Promethean Faust, no Vautrin he, no Camusian rebel—only the day-to-day fret of the social conformist, as distinguished from the cosmic yawp of the existential rebel. Colonel Cathcart's *Angst* is that of the *kleine Mensch* whose ambition to embody his society's ideals is continually frustrated by his failure to understand its rules, who constantly seeks integration with what forever eludes him. The first modern protagonists to exhibit these symptoms of complacency and insecurity were the passive heroes of Scott's Waverley Novels. Edward Waverley, Frank Osbaldistone, Harry Bertram, and Nigel Olifaunt—to name several —are paradigms of "rehearsed responses" to society's construct of values, to law and order, prudence and restraint. The Waverley hero is the contrary of the romantic hero. He seeks accommodation with, rather than revolt against, the bureaucratic, the official, and the academic. He is a forerunner of the twentieth-century functionary, bent on submission of his thoughts to the notions-counter beliefs of a mass culture.

The Scott hero, according to Alexander Welsh's perceptive analysis,[1] strives to identify himself with a code of behavior derived not from reality but from the eighteenth-century legal abstraction of property rights. He could still count, however, on a decaying class system firmly based on the actuality of the landed aristocracy. His counterpart in the twentieth century also finds law and order, stability and prudence, desirable; but in today's supermarket culture, he is less certain of what constitutes law and order, for the stock beliefs of a corporational society are even more beset by the winds of fashion and the chimeras of abstraction than were agrarian societies in the past. Group values—manners, economic, political, and social ideals—rarely originate or evolve naturally. They derive from arbitrary assertions of the social will that must be learned— with few guidelines available or helpful in this continual confrontation, other than trial and error. Hence, to know what society wishes of one is an uncertain business, and to sublimate one's desires to its goals a frustrating experience, particularly when "getting on" is the chief principle. Coleridge characterized the world of the Waverley Novel as one "of *anxiety* from the crown to the hovel, from the cradle to the coffin." "All is an anxious straining to maintain life, or *appearances*," he adds, "to *rise* as the only condition of not falling."[2] This brilliant ascription of what ails the society of the Waverley Novels also defines the malaise of Colonel Cathcart's world of the forties, in which Auden saw anxiety as the spirit of the age. The anxious Gogolian figure of Colonel Cathcart finds his latter-day social role much more difficult to assume than did the Waverley hero, for the world since Scott's day has accelerated its drift toward fragmentation of experience, isolation of the individual, irrelevancy of the future, and sense of personal inadequacy.

Scott's fictional world of landowning squirearchy presents an appearance of stability and cohesion that did not accord exactly with reality. Scott's age was in transition from an agrarian to an urban society. The traditional hierarchy of values, orderly and unchanging, was crumbling before cultural innovations and accelerating social mobility, terrestrial equivalents to the new world-picture of an organic, ever-expanding universe. Epistemologically, man found himself separated from both the phenomenal and noumenal worlds he inhabited, with only his erring sensibility as a link between him and the outside. The sense of security of the Wordsworth of 1797 to 1807 derives from his belief in man's capacity to bridge the gap between perceiving mind and object perceived and hence in the meaningful relation of man to his environment. But beneath even his calm assertion of order lurked a haunting fear of the old chaos, of flux, and the abdication of authority, which slowly eroded his faith in the transcendental self. This instability Scott defines culturally and historically in terms of the romantic lawlessness of the Highlands and of the hopeless cause of the Jacobites; but by whatever name he gives it, the involvement of his passive hero in its disturbing milieu reflects the crisis of consciousness of his time—and of ours.

Since the advent of the Waverley hero, society has become increasingly diffuse and contradictory. What was originally a crisis in political economy, complicated by epistemological symptoms, has deepened into a full-blown metaphysical malaise, for in this century society has become a version of the void. This disorientation of society poses new problems for the passive hero, who seeks to realize the authenticity of his self through his identification with its commonplaces. To offset the drift toward entropy, toward chaos, "the black and vasty zephyrs of the Pit," as Ebenezer Cooke more than once characterizes the philosophical vacuum that stares him in the face (*The Sot-Weed Factor*, III, 13), today's common man looks to the newest electronic devices for ways of holding together the disintegrating center of experience in some semblance of order. In place of the ordering logic of cause and effect, he substitutes the organizing ratio of average and mean. But in his eagerness to be average, he submits to a code of behavior more determinedly abstract than that of the Waverley hero. How else account for the nightmarish nature of Colonel Cathcart's world or the unreality of Eliot Rosewater's sojourn with the ordinary folk living on the ancestral preserve of Rosewater County, Indiana, in *God Bless You, Mr. Rosewater*.

America at mid-century is the product of a generation of statistician's graphs. It has evolved into a computer society, vividly dramatized in the animate-inanimate ambiguities of Thomas Pynchon's *V.* "Me and SHOCK are what you and everybody will be someday," the robot SHROUD ("synthetic human, radiation output determined") gibes at Benny Profane (ch. 10). SHROUD is "five feet nine inches tall—the fiftieth percentile of Air Force standards." Contrived of a skeleton that had once belonged to a living human, it is covered with clear cellulose acetate butyrate, its lungs, sex organs, kidneys, thyroid, liver, spleen and other internal organs designed to measure the amount of radiation which the human body can safely absorb. From Gallup Poll estimates to insurance actuary tables, as Pynchon notes, all aspects of life are being geared to a mythical average without flesh and bone, an average that consists of no living object, no actual person. To serve society's utilitarian end of the collective good, the passive hero has submitted his consciousness of self to a true abstraction.[3] The "century's man," like Herbert Stencil in *V.*, he has altered himself into "something which does not exist in nature" (ch. 8). The Waverley hero as a symbol of his society's ideal of the sacred inviolability of property could not act aggressively because of the necessary submission of his will to the principle of law which protects property. The Black Humor hero as an embodiment of this century's worship of the average cannot relate to any individual because of the reduction of his being to a contrived ratio which renders the extremes of personality nonexistent. Hence the *Angst* of his situation, symbolized by the Soldier-in-White in *Catch-22*, who is believed by the other patients of the hospital not even to exist beneath his all-enveloping bandages. Indeed, the world of *Catch-22* exhibits the *ne plus ultra* of man as ratio, epitomized in Colonel Cathcart's all-purpose letters of condolence to a dead airman's family. In life the flier had existed to the military bureaucracy as an entry on a roster list; in death he fades to an undiscriminated category, "father-son-husband-nephew-brother," which is forwarded to the bereaved for checking off the right relationship. Similar red tape dictates that a dead man's personal effects linger on a bed in Yossarian's tent, because their owner had gotten himself killed before he could report in as a replacement. If he was never added to the squadron roster, bureaucratic logic dictates, he cannot now be removed from it. Doc Daneeka suffers a like fate. Since his name is on the flight manifesto of a plane that crashed, he is officially described as dead, although he continues to walk about the camp as an embarrassing corpus delicti of the reductive transformation of man into mean.

Surely it is what one might with some validity call a dissociation of the average which accounts, in part, for the current alienation of so many in the under thirty age group. The national norm continues to be sustained by a dream of material success. For most of the history of this country its work ethic has functioned well enough as a conditioner of national attitudes, mainly because life goals of the last three centuries, whether in the coastal cities or on the back roads, differed little from those of western societies of the past three thousand years. Ours was a survival society, its goals food, clothing, and shelter sufficient to sustain life. To attain such ends, industry, fortitude, reliability, and honesty usually proved most satisfactory in the long run. Since the end of the Second World War, however, the spectre of scarcity for most people has been eliminated. And for the underprivileged remnants of the population a welfare system has evolved which supplies the traditional necessities. The cost of this economy of plenty fiscally is fairly well understood; but the price we must pay in ways other than in dollars and cents—not only in a perpetual wartime alert and in an ecological crisis, but in changes in our habits of mind[4]—has not yet been adequately assessed.

From a country of sectional differences and local identities, we have metamorphosed into a highly complex technological society of interchangeable parts, of vast megapolises stretching the lengths of both coasts. Collective conformity—a likeness of industry, town, and suburb—attests to our managerial organization, but also to our national submission to new faceless roles. "Mass culture and mass communication," Roger Price notes irreverently in *The Great Roob Revolution* "are standardizing Americans, but they are not unifying us."[5] "The entrapments of collectivism," Jerzy Kosinski, the author of *The Painted Bird*, has called television and radio ("which permeate our privacy and destroy the aloneness out of which it becomes possible to learn to build a self"), drugs ("which smash the mirror of personal identity"), stereophonic rock music, the featureless suburbs, and the educational machine. All permit the individual to escape direct contact with the self or with others. The time honored words expressing the desire to define "Who am I?" now mean to the new conformist "Who do they want me to be?" The phrase "Doing one's own thing" merely mocks its speaker's desire to be part of "an amorphous supergang."[6] On all sides today one hears that "he is certainly entitled to his opinion"—a luxury in the history of man seldom permitted, yet invoked now with a persistence and faith that is testament to the need to believe in its possibility as much as in its likelihood.

No individual today can believe romantically that he still controls his fate when at any time a nervous functionary or an electronic failure can start an atomic holocaust. The new thrusts of those under thirty—the first to never know a survival, goal-oriented environment—are toward role playing and identity achievement. If in the past we realized a sense of ourselves in terms of the traditional values of western civilization and in terms of family and community, in the present this identification must increasingly be realized in relation to other people—at a time when one is more coerced by collective machinery than ever before. One's sense of self has become unfixed. It varies with the role one adopts as one moves from group to group. Personality, as television daily tells us, can be altered by changing the model of our car, the tint of our hair, the brand of our mouth wash. "You may become whatever you desire," Lester Jefferson recalls the drugstore prophet assuring him in the form of a bottle of Silky Smooth. "Perhaps I'd even become a politician or a preacher," he fantasies, patting his hair straightened and dyed yellow to disguise his being a black American (*The Wig*, ch. 8). The inner man is equivalent to his external appearance, which in turn is the sum of the interchangeable products he uses. In a society beset by a dissociation between dated ideals and immediate reality, between the myth of individuality and the submission to anonymity, between the desire to be an instrumental member of a group and the pressure to fit within every statistical mean, there unavoidably engenders tension and anxiety. It is an anxiety different from the old hungers that once assailed man; and the Black Humor of the sixties is, in part, a literary response to it.

Scott compounds the anxiety of his hero by transporting him out of the familiar ethos of Georgian England with its great country houses and law-abiding stable citizenry across the border into Stuart Scotland with its Highland ferocity and anarchic warrior class. This prototypical journey into an alien environment figures in much Black Humor literature. One thinks of Humbert Humbert's motel-haunted trips of discovery across continental America in Nabokov's *Lolita*, of Stern's terrifying nightly walk home from the bus stop after moving from the ghetto security of the city to the suburbs in Friedman's *Stern*, and of Les and Little Jimmie's contretemps with the cab driver in a ride from Harlem downtown to Broadway and 52nd Street in Charles Wright's *The Wig*. By mid-twentieth century, the abstraction of society has proceeded so far that a fictional hero need not travel to foreign lands to find himself surrounded by indifferent people, unable to communicate with anyone, uncertain even about who he is.

This journey motif dramatizes the identity crisis, which afflicts mid-century's *l'homme maudit*, bereft even of a sense of his own authenticity. Both Stern and Lester Jefferson as Jewish and Black Americans are reduced to pseudo-existences in ecumenical America. Theirs is the excruciating pain of not feeling themselves to be fully

97

defined individuals. And their initiations into adult responsibility, toward which the narrative of each novel is largely directed, symbolize their efforts on the psycho-sexual level to assume new social roles. The grammar of current Black Humorists, however, holds that no complete metamorphosis of being is possible, wittily parsed in the inexhaustible puns on places and persons—epitomized by the mythical *Vheissu* (*wie heisst du*? or what is your name?)—in Pynchon's *V*. Hence such Black Humor characters as Stern and Lester are doomed to subsist dietarily on the endless anxiety of personal incompleteness and social ostracism.

In a world which sets great store on conformity, clothes acquire transcendent value. Dress is a desperate concern of the Waverley hero. It determines the treatment accorded to others and received in return. Clothes allow one to distinguish the collective stance from romantic gestures of disruptive lawlessness. God-fearing, upright Jeanie Deans in *The Heart of Midlothian*, is treated with suspicion as disreputable and hence a threat to order when Maud Wildfire drags her dusty and bedraggled into church. Frank Osbaldistone, in *Rob Roy*, nervously frets about his appearance when he arrives travel-worn at the country house of his uncle; and he reacts with moral bewilderment to Diane Vernon's disheveled loose-flowing dress at their first meeting. Scott carefully identifies his madmen by their outlandish garb.

It is not unsignificant then nor wholly accidental that Friedman in a contemporary treatment of mass manners should have his characters lament the disappearance of this traditional social sign. The uniformity of dress in today's mass society prevents Stern from knowing how to act, complicating his uncertain *rapprochement* to people. In the Air Force everyone wears the same uniform, making fliers and nonfliers, Jews and Gentiles, look alikes. On the commuter train everyone is garbed in the same indistinguishable businessman's grey. At the Grove Rest Home the ubiquitous bathrobe and slippers effectively camouflage personal differences. One might expect that Stern would welcome a uniformity which gives him a cheap purchase on participation in the group; but the conformity of contemporary society, like the modern conglomerate, presents an artificial, even false unity, a heterogeneity masquerading as homogeneity. Beneath the sameness of masks riots the old racial disorders and psychic stresses, posing for the eager conformist the bated breath and uncertainly of misstep. No wonder then that Stern is upset because "there was no way to tell by looking" that his employer Belavista had $3,000,000. "He might have been a man with $300,000 or even $27,500, and Stern felt if you had millions, there ought to be a way for people to tell this at a glance. A badge you got to wear or a special millionaire's necktie" (p. 89).

Charles Wright parodies the opposite situation, the plight of Lester, whose impersonations of the white man downtown are betrayed by his black skin. Beneath his masquerades remains always the same self-deprecating American Negro, sold on the promises of the Great Society but frustrated in his effort to join it. With savage laughter *The Wig* depicts the same fixed situation plaguing Lester's acquaintances. Nonnie Swift's impersonation of a Creole from New Orleans, Mrs. Tucker's of a Carolina plantation aristocrat, the Deb's of a Junior Leaguer, Little Jimmie's of a movie star and song and dance entertainer—all are acceptable roles in the Great Society and all are beyond them, Harlem blacks indistinguishable from each other in every respect but their fantasied desires.

A breakdown in communication has accompanied the loss of a sense of personal authenticity. Ironically, the goal sought—conformity as the acme of normality—has rendered the individual more vulnerable and isolated than ever before. Disturbed by this unexpected fact, ordinary man recoils paradoxically from the sober prudence of society in favor of the coherence of self. He becomes the hippy making his scene all alone. Sebastian Dangerfield in Donleavy's *The Ginger Man* is the conformist hero turned inside out, a conformist *manqué*, in raging protest against the uniformity of the bourgeois values he exploits. His is a rascally parody of the ultra-respectable citizen, with excellent credit rating.[7] Samson Sillitoe in Elliot Baker's *A Fine Madness* is similarly parodic of the romantic poet, goaded into resistance to the conformist regimen of the utilitarian world. They are the end product of the romantic assertion of self in a liberal tradition, which posits as its standard the greatest good for the greatest number. Both are mass men, who choose isolation because they recognize it as the inadvertent consequence of mass accommodation. But, as Sebastian is constantly learning to his discomfort, man cannot dissociate himself entirely

99

from the world. Unfortunately now, however, when a Stern, a Lester Jefferson, or a Sebastian Dangerfield seeks to relate to another, he speaks out of the fixed solipsism of his own jerry-built scene. He is an imprisoned I, an integer absorbed by the penchant for the average, lacking in the skill or will to contact a Thou. Rather than addressing an individual in a meaningful meld of sensibilities, he talks past the person. The irrelevancy of such converse confirms his dread of dislocation and increases his sense of anxiety. The obliquity of dissonance rather than the union of confrontation prevails.

Much of the laughter of disquiet in Friedman's writing derives from this dramatic situation. Home from the doctor's, where an examination has disclosed an ulcer, Stern finds his mother and father there but his wife out. "Isn't your wife home when you have an ulcer?" his mother asks incongruously, as if ulcers came and went with the regularity of the evening meal or with the frequency of headaches. "She doesn't know about it yet," Stern replies. Automatically, as if the exchange between Stern and his mother had not occurred, his father chimes in, "She ought to be home if you're not feeling well" (p. 108). Such scenes occur frequently in the pages of Friedman's stories. They are the ordinary currency of his people's lives. Worried about getting into college, Joseph asks his mother for advice. She answers, "The money will be there." "I don't mean that. I don't know which ones to send off to," he replies. "Don't worry about the money," she continues, "We'll get it somehow. It'll be there" (p. 10). The multiplication of Joseph's uncertainty after his talk with his mother is understandable. Her assurance has increased rather than lessened his distress. Words, a bridge linking one person to another, have served only to widen the breach between Joseph's adolescent problem and her adult misunderstanding of it. Friedman dramatizes the generation gap here; even more profoundly, he demonstrates how uniformity, the ideal of the social conformist, is self-defeating, limiting man to the caprice of his own locked-in sensibility. Such communal isolation is at the roots of both Stern's and Joseph's anxiety.

The isolation of Lester's world derives less from the disjunctions of social conformity, although that also occurs, than from the distortions of racial myth and stereotype. The image of the white man

Lester tries to impersonate belongs to the folklore of America, not to the reality of the situation, to the Horatio Alger myth of working one's way up the ladder of success, from porter to bank president (cf. ch. 5), and to the white stereotype of the American Negro as a happy-go-lucky lover of watermelon and sleep in the shade, shift-less, contented with things as they are, full of soul, and naturally rhythmical and sunny dispositioned (cf. ch. 7). As the cab driver taking Lester and Little Jimmie to a recording session says, "Never knew a colored person that didn't have a fine singing voice" (ch. 7). A contrary stereotype to the Uncle Tom, also current, which complicates Lester's frantic quest for a role which will usher him into the Great Society, is the belief that the placid mask of the Black American hides "a natural killer," an over-sexed, pot-smoking cop-hater. That Lester seems to accept these various roles, assum-ing one after another, points not only to his radical lack of identity but also to his and his friends' mistaking these stereotypes for real identities. In the endless impersonations of Lester and company, Charles Wright gives us a comic rendering of the Black American's disenfranchisement from the human race; but in the symbolism of Lester's glorious yellow "wig," thanks to the patented chemicals of the drug industry, and in the theme of the American Dream that every boy may occupy the White House (even a black man by the year 2000 Lester dreams, ch. 1) and its counter Nightmare of pre-tence, Wright underscores how much an assemblage of props and falsehoods, yet another product in a consumer economy, is the con-formist protagonist in a conformist society, how much he is both a statistical sum of social abstractions and a packaged product of his consumer economy.

II

The aesthetic strategies that a world picture at sixes and sevens has elicited from today's artists, who would honestly make sense of contemporary life, have been ingenious and brilliant, if some-times bewildering. The stagings of Happenings and Environments are attempts to give artistic expression to a world of becoming, in which successive instants smack more of contingency than of cau-

101

sality. Thus, unlike Absurd drama, the Happening celebrates the world's complexity. It differs from Black Humor, however, in its forcing the participant to perform the task usually done by the artist, that is, to structure "that part of perception which belongs to the receiver."[8] According to its originator, Allan Kaprow, the Happening (especially within an Environmental situation) is an analogue, raised to aesthetic importance, of the "responsible act" of the Existentialist.[9] Since the Happening then insists on a choice of action, it represents a selection by exclusion from the many possibilities of life; hence it offers basically an alternative ordering of unstructured multiplicity in contrast to that of Black Humor's gesture at exhaustion of all the possibilities. More pertinent to our understanding of Black Humor's search for ways of translating contemporary anxieties into aesthetic terms are the temporal and spatial innovations of certain other Pop artists, Abstract-Expressionist painters, and Environmental sculptors.

Coleridge said that Scott lacked imagination, that faculty which is creative and hence synthetic in function, a maker of unities, a bestower of spatial, temporal, and causal order in the world. Scott is unable to conceive character as an inwardly complex agent out of whose complexity evolves the event and the destiny, but sees it as a product of circumstances and accidents.[10] Without accusing them of a similar absence of imagination, one can note that many contemporary artists exhibit the same abeyance of imaginative cohesion, despite their multiform shifts to escape through non-naturalistic styles from a universe of dimension in space and time, which is the condition of flux and change (and hence of anxiety) and with which they presently feel no harmonious relationship. "Presenting objects in depth," according to Joseph Frank in "Spatial Form in Modern Literature," "gives them a time-value . . . because it connects them with the real world in which events occur."[11] Joseph Frank is paraphrasing and interpreting Wilhelm Worringer's *Abstraktion und Einfühlung* (1908), who with Germanic philosophical fervor is bent on formulating an aesthetico-psychological principle which explains the continual alternation between naturalistic and non-naturalistic styles. The questionable historicism aside, Worringer's theory does pinpoint why many contemporary artists, both plastic and literary, have "moved to overcome, so far as possible, the time-elements involved in their perception."[12] The paradox of their strategy, however, is that although dimension, which is intrinsic to linear arts, is suspended in much modern painting, the condition of time continues to force itself upon our awareness—and to remind us of the potential continuity of existence. With great inventiveness the contemporary artist poses an arrested world of flattened, integrated objects that suggest a transitional universe, in which harmonious relationships are missing. In this respect he has moved beyond the simplistic representation of experience implied in Wilhelm Worringer's theory, as paraphrased by Frank, that the disappearance of depth in a non-naturalistic style also involves the absence of time-elements. Paradoxically these artists are striving to reconfirm the self-contained individuality of things (as with the Pop painters), while continuing to evoke the modern sense of disequilibrium between man and nature and the incohesion between man and events. Not for nothing have these dichotomous art forms been largely indigenous in this century to America, classless, restless, and transitional from the gasoline to electronics age.

The tactics of the monotonously multiplied silk-screen images of an Andy Warhol portrait are obvious. Wittier demonstrations of the tension of time are the humble household objects of Claes Oldenburg, swollen to larger than life size and softened into lumpily stuffed vinyl, that sag wearily, forcing upon our awareness the precariousness of existence. Similar uses of commonplace subjects form the staple of William Kienholz' and George Segal's sculptures. Kienholz' constructions of a lunch-room counter or of a mental-ward cell suspend time in an ominous reminder of its inexorability. Segal's bland plaster figures ironically parody life-like scenes that reek of death, of the arrest of motion.

More dynamically expressive images of contingency, which are heroic because they have not succumbed to solipsism, are the monumental black on white struggles of Franz Kline's paintings.[13] Black brush strokes expand outward, pushing and extending the perimeter of their energy until they have enough space in which to move and breathe, with light and dark locked in a tension of borders held at bay. The same vague threat to continuity informs the ominously expanding-contracting lines of Nicholas Krushenick's pictures.[14] One cannot be certain whether the configuration of caterpillar-like stripes and cloud-like billows are pulling back to free the patterned linear stripes beneath or spreading to engulf them. Hence the blatant optimism of Krushenick's candy-cane colors masks a movement of menace that refuses to be contained, but breathes and distends beyond the edges of the canvas and by implication out into the environment.

Similar apocalyptic hostility characterizes the precarious world of Roy Lichtenstein's comic-strip inventions. The narrative movement of his picture spills over its literal boundaries, suggestive of continuing action; yet its actual outcome is never known, for it remains only one unit of a potential comic strip of multiple units. The resultant sense of what Frank Kermode has called the "purely successive, disorganized time" of "the interval between *tock* and *tick*"[15] receives additional support from the dissynchronism of the human figure's words and movements. As if these witty inventions were not enough for conveying the disequilibrium with nature and the incohesion with events of the individual caught in an unfinished present that, like the world of Nabokov's *Ada*, is without past or future, Lichtenstein is drawn to a subject matter of arrested transition, of a single woman sinking into an horizonless sea or turning away from the viewer toward the nothingness of the undefined interior perspective, of a soldier confronting the limitless action of battle, or of a flier crowding the borders of the canvas with his airplane, as if in vain escape from the flattened space behind him. The primary reds and yellows of the Sunday comics further stamp these figures indifferently with anonymity.

The desire to control the temporality inherent in literary form, for purposes analogous to those of the paintings considered, has been pronounced in Black Humor. The language of Sebastian Dangerfield, in *The Ginger Man*, its sentences truncated of subjects and verbs, eclipses philistinic belief in the continuity and consequent moral responsibility of one's actions, pinpointing instead with disturbing insouciance the still point of a nacreous present. The juxtaposition of events separated by fifty years, with the early *opéra bouffe* occurrences superimposed arbitrarily as a meaningful force onto the immediate moment, in *V.*, hallucinates ordinary faith in

104

the logic of history, transforming its determinism into willful constructs of the human mind. The parodic catenation of epochs and literary styles in *The Sot-Weed Factor* and *Giles Goat-Boy* and the *déjà vu* of *Catch-22* fix time in endless repetition, which questions the accepted view of its linearity and its truth. The journeys of Humbert Humbert with his nymphet across the continental U.S.A., in *Lolita*, attempt to coerce the living present into a representation of the dead past, by subsuming the temporally incomplete self in the geographical and cultural ambience of a nation, as well as in the impossible physical and spiritual stasis of a girl's nymphancy. In *Ada* Nabokov resolutely violates space and time, blurring national and continental boundaries and handling the chronology of technical innovation for the ninety year period from 1870 to 1960 with deliberate anachronism. He even composes for Van Veen, the protagonist, a treatise attempting to dismiss temporal succession as normally experienced. Interestingly, Nabokov's exercise in the meaning of Time parallels the earlier effort of Borges in "A New Refutation of Time" (1944–46) to deny the self and "the irreversible and iron-clad" river of time by means of the gamesmanship of words.

The pace of a scientific and technical society has fallen out of phase with man's traditional time sense. His inner time clock as well as the ticking of his cultural time table no longer coincide with social change. One consequence has been the increased tension of urban existence and of twentieth-century life. Friedman's fiction faithfully renders the bewildered impulse of the modern consciousness. His prose has a brash bounciness and nervous tempo, which catches faithfully the "near hysterical new beat in the air" that is the mid-century idiom of our culture, with its stereoscopic and stereophonic dance halls, amplified discotheques, scheduled love-ins, bare-bosomed waitresses, and neon-lit nights—what Friedman in the Foreword to *Black Humor* calls the "punishing isolation and loneliness of a strange, frenzied new kind."[16] His language, comparable to Krushenick's candy-cane colors and Lichtenstein's bland comic-strip technique, is bare of pretense, recklessly vulnerable to the sneer of sophistication. Its nakedness, its impetuous innocence, underscores the morbid anxiety that the conformist hero imbibes daily with his morning coffee. Here is Joseph's father in a speech that summarizes the fears of the parent telling his child about the

105

facts of life in the space age, related in the defiant, bullying manner of the addict of the commonplace. He is taking Joseph to the airport, where he will fly to Kansas to attend college.

> Riding down in the elevator, Joseph's father said, "Now do you know where you're going?"
> "To college," said Joseph. "Is that what you mean?"
> "Now, I'm not fooling around," his father said, "I just want to make sure you've got your head screwed onto your shoulders. You know, sometimes you do some funny things. Like putting on your pants first, tightening them and then trying to jam your shirt in through the belt. You won't be able to do things like that out there. You'll get sent home and you'll be damned sorry, get what I mean? . . .
> At the airport Joseph's father asked him if he had ever been on a plane. "Well, that's something to think about," he said. "How do you know you're going to like it?"
> "I don't Dad," said Joseph.
> "Well, there you are, you've saved this for the last second. A lot of people get up there and they find they don't care for flying. They get nauseous. What are you going to do then? Look, I can't run your life. If that happens, tell your mother, and the people on the plane will get you something. They must have something for people in that condition. What the hell, the airlines are big business today. You act as though you're the first person ever flew a plane." (pp. 192, 194)

His fiction underscores in its structural conception the *non sequitur* of current human actions. For him, events are ultimately motiveless, the line between fantasy and reality, thought and occasion, impression and object, continually wavering and blurring. That they happen, not why, becomes central. Hence Friedman concentrates on the rich texture of surface details. His individuals, like the Scott hero as defined by Coleridge, lack the inward complexity, the self-consciousness, which could relate the events of their lives to a larger frame of social reference. Instead they are at any given moment the two-dimensional embodiment of circumstance and accident. Thus they are fixed in being, yet constantly in motion. In adolescent echo of his father's feeble thrust for awareness, Joseph is inclined much of the time to conceive of his life in terms of arrested stills of great cinema moments. The fixed narrative continuity of the movies represents for him the ultimate achievement or order in his worried effort to give meaning to his inchoate experience. Thus he nervously wonders, after learning that Columbia University has turned down his application for admission, "why he could react to tragedy only with movie routines. Now he was the high school hero caught stealing exam answers on the eve of the big game, waiting outside the principal's office to see whether he would be allowed to compete against State" (p. 71). Seeing a "slender blond woman, whose body seemed all pressed out beneath her slacks," he decides that she has that "whimpering look to her face as though a young, handsome rogue had just run out of her starved and loveless mansion . . . a whipped Barbara Stanwyck style" that he knew "he was going to find attractive later in life" (p. 38).

Like the stopped action of a Lichtenstein picture, *Stern* and *A Mother's Kisses* consist of incidents that either end inconclusively or lack coherence between person and event, thought and action. Stern's ulcer and nervous breakdown wax out of all proportion to the insult his wife receives from a neighbor. At the conclusion, by way of avenging his wife's dishonor, he sustains a beating by the man; so his anxiety flourishes as usual. Similarly, nothing is meaningfully concluded in Joseph's world, whether it is his aborted stay as a waiter at a summer camp, his affliction with a mysteriously infected arm, or his fantastic "temporary" lodgement in a hotel room as prerequisite to his registering for college classes. The absurd disjunction between the archaic human timetable and the juggernaut of civilization's calendar is dramatized in Stern's inability to synchronize his recognition of the need to paint his house and to spray his shrubbery against insects with the "printed" instructions about when the chemical products must be used for maximum effectiveness. Consequently his house remains unpainted and his shrubs are decimated by caterpillars.

Friedman's world is ominously dependent on chance, a world of inconsequential meetings and partings. The future ceases to exist as an estimable series of actions. The categories of time and space fail to define the limits of perception, leaving Stern and Joseph forever vulnerable to the indefinites of unfolding experience. As in the involved world of television defined by Marshall McLuhan, so in the would-be conformist worlds of *Stern* and *A Mother's Kisses* discontinuity and simultaneity have displaced uniformity and consecutiveness. Hence the absence in Friedman's stories of family history, of sense of place, of names (what is Stern's first name? Joseph's last? Joseph's father's?), of anything other than the rudiments of narrative succession; and contrariwise an emphasis on the terrifying involutions of the moment. Under the circumstances not to feel anxiety is not to be human.

Charles Wright similarly depicts the Harlem of his protagonist in *The Wig* as undefined by either its past or by its geography. Lester's silky-smooth hair, apotheosized as the wig, indicates to us the central emphasis of his world. It is product oriented and medium directed. Lester's mind is a grab bag of popular commercial slogans:

> Do not the auburn-haired gain a new sense of freedom as a blonde (see *Miss Clairol*)? Who can deny the madness of a redesigned nose (see *Miami Beach*)? The first conference of Juvenile Delinquents met in Riis Park and there was absolutely no violence: a resolution was passed to send Seconal, zip guns, airplane glue, and contraceptives to the Red Chinese (see *The Daily News*). The American Medical Association announced indignantly that U. S. abortion and syphilis quotas are far below the world average (see *Channel 2*). Modern gas stations have coin-operated air pumps in the ladies' room so the underblessed may inflate their skimpy boobs (see *Dorothy Kilgallen*). . . . Schizo wisdom? Remember, I said to myself, you are living in the greatest age mankind has known. (ch. 1)

Lester's life has no continuity. It is as fragmented as the one-minute spot commercials on television. Part of the life stream of the nation in its submission to seeking out and partaking of the great national barbecue, his life shares in none of its history, in none of the explanation of or contribution to the isolated, inconclusive one-liners of advice—labels with instructions on how to use the product—which add up to a day in the life of the mid-century American consumer.

The disjunction between his effort to act "white" and his shaky grasp of the nuances of the role provides the novel with its chief tension. As Lester recognizes, "Impersonation is an act of courage, as well as an act of skill, for the impersonator must be cold-hearted, aware of his limitations." Yet his next thought is that he "*had* no limitations," that he was "Apollo's Saturday morning son."

108

The new image he pictures himself as filling, based on his silky-smooth wig, is aristocratic:

> I found myself at 1 p.m. alighting from a chauffer-driven Silver Cloud Rolls-Royce on Sutton Place South. In my 14th Street-Saville Row suit (dark, synthetic, elegant) that I'd bought from Mr. Fishback—I was truly *together*. And the six joints of Haitian marijuana I'd smoked on the way down made me feel powerful. Like Cassius Clay. Like Hitler. Like Fats Domino. Like Dick Tracy. (ch. 9)

And how had Lester managed this temporary transformation? By the tried-and-true system of "an all purpose, fake forged Credit Card, guaranteed at five hundred hospitals in all fifty states. Honored instantly by one thousand fine hotels and restaurants, plus major service stations, and airlines. Car-rental agencies also guaranteed." Not to buy on credit is Un-American. In its most superficial form Les has joined the American main stream. Yet the inauthenticity—the Dick Tracy ersatz quality—of his act is pathetically evident. It is the act of a member of an inchoate black people trying with the hand-me-down manners of an obsolete South and the supermarket customs of an anonymous North to define himself according to the ethos of an evolving white middle-class world. In a skillful fusion of theme and form, the discontinuity of Lester's life is paralleled by an absence of narrative sequence. For Lester, as for the novel, the hours of the day and days of the week and weeks of the year are an unconnected succession of aborted masquerades: "like a young man in a four-color ad" (ch. 3), episodes of make-believe that begin in hopes and dreams and end in the reality of a "wafer-thin stomach," "the smell of bacon grease and burnt toast," *The New York Times Directory of Employment Agencies*, and always another morning in Harlem (chs. 1, 11, 14, 16). Not to be "a desperate man" (ch. 1) is not to have to go on breathing in the gray dawn of each of those mornings.

III

Stern and Lester Jefferson are no rebels against the establishment. They are "law and order" boys. As if their status as mid-century cyphers and functionaries was not enough to undermine their self-confidence, their anxieties are compounded by the civil violences of their urban existence. Their neuroses are the special ones of minority races living in a dominant White-Anglo-Saxon-Protestant community. But one does not have to nudge the language very hard to recognize in their anxieties the terrors of ineffectuality felt in common by mass man in the twentieth century. Like so many ordinary citizens today, who acquiesce to illegality and crime because they do not wish to get involved with the law, Stern looks upon the police as potential enemies not upholders of law and order. He is afraid to call them to protect him against his neighbors. He pictures them as "large, neutral-faced men with rimless glasses who would accuse him of being a newcomer making vague trouble-making charges" (p. 30). He is suspicious of justice meted out by commissioners and judges. He worries about offending the local firemen, fearful that they might turn "deliberately sluggish," letting his house burn to the ground, while playing "weak water jets on the roof, far short of the mark" (p. 25). With bitter irony that eventually strikes back at itself, Lester alludes to the police on 125th Street:

> New York's finest were on the scene, wearing custom-made Chipp uniforms, 1818 Brooks Brothers shirts, Doctor U space shoes (bought wholesale from a straw basket in Herald Square). A pacifistic honor guard, twelve policemen per block, ambitious night sticks trimmed with lilies of the valley, WE ARE OUR BROTHER'S KEEPER buttons illuminating sharp-brimmed Fascist helmets—they bow to each fast-moving Harlemite from crumby Lenox to jet-bound Eight Avenue. (ch. 4)

Little Jimmie reacts paranoically at the sight of them. Disgusted with Jimmie's fears, Lester reassures himself that "The policemen were our protectors, knights of the Manhattan world. I wasn't afraid. I was goddam grateful." "The cops are our friends," he tells Jimmie. "Then why do we have to run?" Jimmie asks. This ambivalence of feeling for society's "soothsayer wearing a dark policeman's uniform . . . twirling his night stick" (ch. 16) is pervasive in the novel.

Ironically in this century the conformist lives in a Kafkan night-

110

mare, incurring apprehension from those same institutions that he turns to for succor. By limiting himself to their bureaucratic order, he hopes to impose a rationale upon his existence. Instead he finds himself paralyzingly isolated, bereft of individuality, a faceless integer who counts simply as a population statistic. If he happens to be like Stern he fails to convince even his wife that he is a person distinguishable from other human beings. When they go up to their second-floor bedroom, she has him go first because she does not "like to go upstairs in front of *people*" (p. 191; my italics). If he is like Lester his humanity is merely a compound of his impersonations. Except for these guises, like Blake's Nobodaddy, he is without being, nonexistent, an invisible man.

Underlying Stern's obsession with the "kike man's" hostility is clearly the larger question of his place in society. Stern is afflicted not only with an ulcer but also with the more psychically virulent American malady of wanting to be liked, of wanting to be accepted as a full-fledged, paid-up member of a group. When he checks out of the Rest Home, he feels "as though by getting healthy he had violated a rotted, fading charter" of the other sicker inmates. "He had come into their sick club under false pretenses, enjoying the decayed rituals, and all the while his body wasn't ruined at all. He was secretly healthy, masquerading as a shattered man so that he could milk the benefits of their crumbling society. And now he felt bad about not being torn up as they were" (p. 158).

As with the Waverley hero, not differentness but sameness is Stern's social goal. In the novel he realizes this ambition only once, on the night he does the town with a local girl and two other inmates of the Rest Home; and his reaction to their togetherness indicates its prime importance for his psychic well-being. They have a fracas in a bar and leave hurriedly before the police arrive. As they jog down the street Stern thinks happily that "they were comrades of a sort and he was glad to be with them, to be doing things with them, to be running and bellowing to the sky at their sides; he was glad their lives were tangled up together. It was so much better than being a lone Jew stranded on a far-off street, your exit blocked by a heavy-armed kike hater in a veteran's jacket" (p. 149).

So urgent is Stern's desire for communal acceptance that it takes precedence over his need to compensate for sexual inferiorities.

Even though he makes love to the Puerto Rican girl and is excited to try it again, he joins forces with the other two boys when they begin to toss her into the air straddled on a broomstick. "Ooh, you really hurt me . . . you cruddy bastards," she cries.

> Stern felt good that she had addressed all three of them, not excluding him, and it thrilled him to be flying out of her apartment with his new friends, all three howling and smacking each other with laughter at the pole episode. He wanted to be with them, not with her. He needed buddies, not a terrible Puerto Rican girl. He needed close friends to stand around a piano with and sing the Whiffenpoof song, arms around each other, perhaps before shipping out somewhere to war. If his dad got sick, he needed friends to stand in hospital corridors with him and grip his arm. He needed guys to stand back to back with him in bars and take on drunks. These were tattered, broken boys, one in a wheelchair, but they were buddies. (p. 156)

A man's sense of identity depends in part on his relationship to the conventional age-groups of his society. Friedman captures the peculiar non-existence of today's Everyman, trapped in an impersonal round of homogenized activities, by portraying him as an American Jew, alienated from Judaic values but as yet unassimilated by American traditions. Thus Stern belongs at least in this respect in the company of the many Jewish fictional heroes of the fifties and sixties. He shares with Bellow's protagonists the disinheritance of the American Jew. At the same time he partakes of the dissociation of the Black Humor protagonist of the sixties. He is both physically part of and mentally apart from the collective community. He lives in it but does not belong to it. He is a non-person, vividly dramatized by his lack of involvement with people. With neither wife, parents, co-worker, employer, friend, nor acquaintances does he successfully communicate.

Stern is driven by the desire to *be* the modern American male. His move from the city to the suburbs, from a Jewish neighborhood to a Gentile community, gives warp to this pattern. Lester is reaching further. He wishes to embody the full myth of being an American. "This was the land of hope and that was it," he exults lying in the darkness before the dawn of a new day. "Sweet brown girl, I'll become a magician for you," he promises, not without its hint of ambivalence however. He has the persistent optimism of a door-to-door salesman. A black Candide, he rebounds from each rebuff certain that the next effort will win him a slurping place at the Money River, as Eliot Rosewater scathingly refers to the wealth of the nation. Thrown out of a recording session at Paradise Records, Ltd., where he had tried to crash in at the top, he decides not unwryly that he "was destined for a higher calling," one which calls for working his way to the top through study and application in the classic American tradition. "Perhaps not Madison Avenue or Wall Street. No. A real man-sized job. A porter, a bus boy, a shoeshine boy, a swing on my father's old Pullman run. Young Abe by the twenty-watt bulb. Sweating, toiling, studying the map of The Great Society. One is not defeated until one is defeated" (ch. 8).

Lester is a true conformist hero in his submissive acceptance of a national ideal. The result is that he becomes little more than an abstraction himself. His inability to get his hands on a slice of the Great Society pie is explained ostensibly by the reality of his situation. The myth he pursues in his fantasies is white. In his infatuation for it he is living white while being black. But his failure also mirrors the unreality of any human attempt to fashion itself after an abstraction. To pattern himself thus is to dehumanize himself. This is an insight Nathanael West dramatized in his satire of the Horatio Alger ideal in *A Cool Million*. It is the renewed insight of the under-thirty rebels against the military-industrial complex that passes in some quarters for America. And it is the Black Humor glimpse into the nonentity of the sixties of Charles Wright in *The Wig*, an updated version of the Algerian confidence game done in black face.

In their efforts to think American, to be aggressive, to be successful, admired by all for their virility, prowess, and savvy, both Stern and Lester are vulnerable. They are never quite able to match their thoughts and actions to their desires. Their uncertain status leaves them shadow-boxing fictitious enemies. Yet real toads do occupy their imaginary gardens. The "kike man" does live down the road; he did shove Stern's wife, whether accidentally or intentionally is never made clear. The mental apprehension of Stern has its real counterpart in the everyday world. Stern walks each moment of his life in a shower of panic, the corrosive acid of fear dogging his foot-

113

steps. His is the centuries-old terror of the Jew living, a minority figure, among pogrom-prone peoples. Alternatively, the Great Society was enunciated by President Johnson as including all the peoples of the United States. Equal opportunity was proclaimed for everyone regardless of race or creed. Yet Lester is always being reminded that "morning all over America" is not the same morning which dawns in Harlem (ch. 16) and that only with "powerful black Negro coffee, spiced with potents," can he "face The White Man come Monday morning" (ch. 11).

Their terror is also representative of this century's terror of the law-abiding citizen living, without visible capacity to control his future, among the irrational forces of nuclear world powers, economic booms and busts, gun-toting Minute Men and Black Panthers, and bomb-throwing Weathermen and head-bashing Hard Hats. Violence is the weathervane of our society. It is the keystone of our ideology, the trademark of our frontier heritage, the drama of our Western mythology, and the epistemology of our Declaration of Independence. Guns are sold, no questions asked, through mail-order houses. Fathers train their sons in good citizenship by giving them a rifle when they come of age. This matter-of-fact acceptance of violence as a cultural ideal is less satirized than parodied in stunned disbelief by Friedman. A pervasive metaphor in the narrative is that of war. Stern's mind and body are portrayed as a no-man's-land populated with the sophisticated hardware of modern combat. He reels continually from actual and imagined blows of civilization. Like Tennyson's "Nature, red in tooth and claw," his ulcer attacks him "coarse-tufted, sharp-toothed" (p. 82). Entire armadas of men and equipment troop into his stomach and bivouack there.

Friedman's nervous prose is highly suggestive of violence. The frequency of active verbs has the fictional characters twitching as energetically and erratically as high-speed, machine-driven marionettes. Henry James's people *swim* into rooms, Friedman's *fly* through them.

No character in modern fiction leads a mental existence more violent than Stern. At every turn of his humdrum round of affairs, he moves like one besieged by superior forces, wary of sudden attacks and skillful murderous incursions into the citadel of his puny

defenses. Clenched fists, military chants, body bursting blows—
every kind of mayhem perfected in this century of violence runs riot
through Stern's impressionable imagination. No one walks, enters,
or exits in Stern's world. He plunges, flies, erupts, bursts. His movements imitate the explosive disruptive forces of violence. Not since
the nineteenth century and the heyday of the Darwinian fever has
man been conceived of as so tremblingly naked before the murderous onslaughts of a hostile environment. Stern must be the most
frightened figure in American fiction, his panic more profound than
the stagey terrors of Brockton Brown's and Poe's heroes, because
ultimately more commonplace and everyday. Perched on the front
steps of his house in the evening, his son on his lap and his great
soft body pressed against his wife's hips for security, Stern feels
jittery and isolated, a disturbing, ill-defined menace surrounding
him. Lost is the paradisal pleasure that was once rural America's of
sitting peacefully on the door stoop to watch the day darken. In the
foreword to his anthology of Black Humor, Friedman comments
on the extremes of today's life. The effect of the bizarre-as-norm on
the man in the street is polarizing: he becomes a frantic Stern or his
antidotal contrary, a representative of "the surprise-proof generation."[17] *Stern* is Friedman's embodiment of this askew world from
the harrassed point of view of one of its reluctant draftees.

Tactics of march and counter-march have filled Stern's mind
since boyhood. As a child he had lived in terror of an orphan boy
whom he imagined would someday "appear suddenly in an alley
with a great laugh, fling Stern against a wall, lift him high, and drop
him down, steal his jacket in the cold, and run away with it, come
back and punch Stern's eyes to slits" (p. 51). His grandmother was
jokingly supposed to have "a whole mob" of other old ladies "organized" (p. 60). His uncles would sing the prayers at Passover as
if they were "militant chants." His Uncle Mackie, with "bronzed,
military-trim body" would do "a series of heroic-sounding but
clashing chants" with "great clangor" as if to "enlist a faction to his
banner and start a split Seder" (pp. 57–58).

As an adult he cowers in abject fear at imaginary reprisals of the
"kike man." He avoids driving past the "kike man's" house, "afraid
that the man would pull him out of the car and break his stomach"
(p. 49). In retaliation Stern dreams of crushing the "kike man"

115

with a blow "battering his head through his living-room window" (p. 102), or of catching the "kike man's" little boy on the bumpers of his car and then driving the mile to his own house in seconds, disappearing undetected into his garage. But the thought of the "kike man's" counterattack paralyzes him.

> He pictured a car fight in which the man would get Stern's boy, following him onto the lawn and pinning him against the drainpipe, while Stern, waiting upstairs, held his hands over his ears, blocking out the noise. The man would then, somehow, pick off Stern's wife in her kitchen and then drive upstairs and finish off Stern himself, cringing in his bedroom. (p. 50)

The "kike man" is named De Luccio. Checking in the telephone book, Stern discovers that there are eighteen other De Luccios in town. Immediately he concedes to himself that even "if he were to defeat the man, an army of relatives stood by to take his place" (p. 50). The sight of the man "wearing a veteran's jacket" makes Stern's throat turn over.

> It meant he had come through the worst part of the Normandy campaign, knew how to hold his breath in foxholes for hours at a time and then sneak out to slit a throat in silence. He was skilled as a foot fighter and went always with deadly accuracy to a man's groin. (pp. 52–53)

And Stern saw the man "a light sleeper, nerves sharpened by combat, waiting, coiled and ready to leap forward and slit throats with commando neatness" (p. 54). In desperation Stern wonders if his being blind, flanked by his wife and child, would protect him from the man's assault, bone-jarring "judo chop" and sickening kick in the crotch (pp. 93–94).

Apart from the contretemps with the "kike man," the normal round of Stern's life is an endless fantasy of cringing self-defense. His assistant at the office, an effeminate young man, always appears to Stern to be darting menacingly, body coiled "with vicious ballet grace," toward his desk. Fearful of being reported to a Board of Good Taste for having an ulcer—a "dirty, Jewish, unsophisticated" malady—Stern longs instead for "dueling scars and broken legs suffered while skiing" (p. 88). He hesitates to admonish a baby sitter for teaching his son about God, "afraid she would come after him one night with a torch-bearing army of gentiles and tie him to a church" (p. 112).

The same fantasy of punitive constraint pursues Stern like a Fury when he goes to the Grove Rest Home. The somber New England air of the place makes Stern-the-good-citizen self-conscious of his Semitic genesis, certain that the founders would veto him "with clenched fists" (p. 115) in spite of his desire to be a loyal American. Informed that milk and cookies are served at five, with only one tardiness allowed, Stern reflects that "even were he to flee to the Netherlands after a milk and cookie infraction, getting a fifteen-hour start," the crippled Negro attendant, with "great jaw muscles," "would go after him Porgy-like and catch him eventually" (p. 117). The patients terrify him, particularly a tall "erupting," "grenade-like youth" whom Stern jumpily keeps expecting to smash him in sudden "swiftly changing mood" (pp. 138–139). When two baseball teams come to the rest home to play a benefit game, Stern excitedly subs for an outfielder hit with a line drive; but at bat, facing the pitcher, he is fearful that a bean ball is "planned to put a bloodflower between his eyes" (p. 141). Sneaking out one night with two other patients for some beers and a tryst with a girl, Stern trembles, certain that the instant they passed the gate the Negro orderly would have them "picked up in trucks and initiate punitive measures" (p. 145). The girl looks like "a battered Puerto Rican caricature of Gene Tierney" "after a session with two longshoremen who'd been paid to rough her up a little, not to kill her but to change her face around a little" (pp. 136, 145).

There is no escape for Stern, no place to hide. Neither convalescence nor work nor home life offers him a haven. He crouches in his office, locks himself in the toilet stall—hiding in uncontrollable panic from the confident steps of his boss in the morning. The phone ring slices at him like a knife. His house awaits him, "an enemy that sucked oil and money and posted a kike-hating sentry down the street" (p. 174). Even in the refuge of his bed, his thoughts are invaded by "numb and choking fear" (p. 173).

Stern lives in a "stifled, desperate" (p. 171) world that knows no primal cause and effect, a world ruled over by a Mosaic dispensation run amok, the Judaic law of an eye for an eye swollen to horrifying, bizarre proportions. Stern dreams of his Negro friend Battleby flinging off his horn-rimmed glasses and filling "an open-cab truck with twenty bat-carrying Negro middle-weights, bare to the waist and glistening with perfect musculature," to do battle with the "kike man" (p. 96). The usual scale of values is tipped into frightening ratios. Man trembles before the accusing eye of a traffic cop, but indulges complacently the excesses and enormities of the Mafia. All the time that he is decrying mass racial extermination, individual cruelty is losing significance.

Stern reacts to the real and imagined dangers of every day with a mental life of sexual aggression and finally in the climactic stages of his nervous breakdown with violent actions. He is the little man on the street, one of the *vox populi* of this century, through whose eyes and ears has been refracted too much violence and pretence. Hollywood and Madison Avenue's exploitation of love as a commodity to be huckstered has left Stern obsessed with sexual nightmares of his wife engaged in "endless, exhausting, intricately choreographed, lovemaking" (p. 162) with her dance instructor. He runs "with teeth clenched through a crowded train station, as though he were a quarterback going downfield, lashing out at people with his elbows, bulling along with his shoulders." To outraged complaints, he hollers, "I didn't see you. You're insignificant-looking" (p. 179). He sasses a traffic cop, lecturing him when stopped for a traffic violation, "Is this your idea of a crime? With what's going on in this country—rape and everything?"

Significantly, Stern's fantasies of fright often revert atavistically to the bare fists of savage reprisal. The friendly handshake has metamorphosed in his daily nightmare into a ubiquitous fist that threatens his existence in crescending multiples. Stern refrains from contradicting a Negro taxi driver, fearful of being backed "against a fender, and cut . . . to ribbons with lethal combinations" (p. 83) of fisticraft. The gentlemanly rules of pugilistic defense do not apply in Stern's imagined world. The Gangland law and senseless rumbles of big city ghettos prevail. Stern's father carries a jagged scar on the ridge of his nose, given to him one day "by two soccer players in a strange neighborhood who had suddenly lashed out and knocked him unconscious" (p. 85). Friends of his father had gone looking for the men with steel piping. A recurrent hallucination of

Stern's depicts him as the victim of ordinary people—drugstore countermen, for example, who suddenly mobilize according to an attack plan and trap Stern in a store against the paperback books, insanely "hitting him in the stomach a few times and then holding him for a paid-off patrolman" (p. 85).

The symbolic action of such hallucinations is obvious. Friedman conceives of man ironically as having regressed to a lawless state in response to an overstructured civilization. The monolithic impersonality of a technocracy communicates to man no sense of his belonging to a group. He has become an outsider, groping in terror for signs that will relate him to his world. Out of a desperate will to survive he slips into a new savagery—a vivid but cruel Alice-in-Wonderland where sadistic Red Queens and Mad Hatters force him, like Alice, continually to reformulate his assumptions about people and manners. The actual has been abandoned for a mental world that more accurately reflects reality. Illogic and mystery have succeeded reason and clarity. "Were you ever a magician before you became my father?" the sexually incompetent Stern is asked by his son. "Right before" (p. 186), Stern answers with the starkness of things seen through the looking-glass.

In *Stern* Friedman portrays the end product of this century's assault on the human sensibility. Man's private and public lives run on separate treadmills these days. A bland noncommittal exterior masks a ferocious fantasy life. Outward acquiescence in a dehumanized society reduces the inner life to catatonic silence or jangling disconnected protest. Stern's affliction is mainly the latter.

The contretemps of *The Wig* follow a different configuration than that of *Stern*, although frustrated conformity continues as a central issue. The major tension of the language of the novel resides in the ambivalent antithesis between the white view of the American Negro and the Black-American view of Whitey. Both contain to a high degree stereotypical attitudes that doom reconciliation and cooperation of the two groups under the rubric of the Great Society or under any other rubric. Hence Lester's masquerade, despite the multiple disguises that it assumes, inevitably fails to realize his goal of acceptance by the larger community. Each of his roles is unrealistic to the extent that it partakes of a stereotype. The unreality is complicated by Lester's belief in the Great Society's promise that

119

all will share equally and uniformly in its benefits, and his acting accordingly, to his continual disappointment. This is why in an author's note, Wright remarks that "the story itself is set in an America of tomorrow." Only then can Lester claim he is "American until the last breath" (ch. 5) and not have expressed "a mirror image" (the subtitle of the novel) of his wish, like Humbert Humbert's dream of possession of Annabel in the person of Lolita.

Concomitant with the succession of roles Lester plays is the shifting point of view. In one speech, at times, may be heard Lester's futuristic confidence that he is part of the American mainstream, his cynical exslave wisdom that remembers generations of lynchings and KKK rule, his acceptance of an image of his race that is the product of white propaganda, and his portrait of the white man that is made up of black militant clichés. Preparing to condition his hair from the "Giant Economy jar of long-lasting Silky Smooth Hair Relaxer, with the Built-in Sweat-proof Base," Lester reads the directions:

> The red, white, and gold label guarantees that the user can go deep-sea diving, emerge from the water, and shake his head triumphantly like any white boy. This miracle with the scent of wild roses looks like vanilla ice cream and is capable of softening in sufficiently Negroid hands.

On the safe side, he adds "Precautionary Oil, thick, odorless, indigenous to the Georgia swamps." Massaging his hair, he remembers that

> old-fashioned hair aids were mixed with yak dung and lye. They burned the scalp and if the stuff got in your eye you could go blind from it. One thing was certain: you combed out scabs of dried blood for a month. But a compassionate Northern Senator had the hair aids outlawed. Said he, in ringing historic words: "Mr. Chairman, I offer an amendment to this great Spade tragedy! These people are real Americans and we should outlaw all hair aids that makes them lose their vibrations and eclat." Silky Smooth (using a formula perfected by a Lapp tribe in Karasjok, Norway) posed no problems.
>
> Yes indeed. A wild excitement engulfed me. My mirrored image reflected, in an occult fashion, a magnificent future. I hadn't felt so good since discovering last year that I actually disliked watermelon.

120

. . . I stood tall like the great-great-grandson of slaves, sharecroppers, Old World royalty. Tall, like a storm trooper, like an Honor Scout. Yes! I'd stalk that druggist if the experiment failed. Lord—it couldn't fail! I'm Walter Mitty's target-colored stepson. Sweet dreams zipped through my mind. A politician had prophesied that it was extremely likely a Negro would be elected President of the United States in the year 2,000. Being realistic, I could just picture myself as Chairman of the Handyman's Union, addressing the Committee on Foreign Relations and then being castrated. (ch. 1)

Surely no recent fictional character leads a more divided mental existence than Lester. And the tension of his conflict in attitudes is underscored by a language of antitheses. Repeatedly his desired image of himself as a white man includes the excoriation of *fascist* and *storm trooper*, while his vision of himself as a black man contains overtones of tom-toms and naked savages swinging from trees. The affluence of an urban consumer society vies in his thoughts with the indigence of an enslaved and marginal rural economy. White power is qualified by black flunkies, the Promised Land with Harlem slums, a pose of man-around-town with a stomach grumbling from two days of fast. The combination of pretense and actuality, haute cuisine and soul food, gentility and seaminess, is epitomized in the parodic chatter of a 125th Street black prostitute who propositions Little Jimmie:

"And we're simply delighted to meet you, Mr. Wishbone, in the flesh. I think we should give those Junior League girls a rain check. Another day for dice and cards and chitchat and Bloody Marys. But I'd be delighted if you'd join me in my study for an informal lunch. I'm a follower of Dione Lucas and James Beard, you know. I'll try to whip up something simple. Kale and turnip greens cooked with juicy ham hocks. Yankee pot roast. German potato salad. Green beans soaked in fat back. And my specialty, cornbread and sweet-potato pie." (ch. 4)

The tone leaps from the literal to the ironic; and the reader is required to hold these contraries in solution. They cannot be resolved in favor of one or another. Lester is not a unified fictional conception in the older novelistic sense of a character with a limited number of personality traits. He is an Uncle Tom, a militant, a sit-

121

lonely terrified individual, a self-hating American Negro, a white American with black face—he is all the roles the Black American plays at some time; he is the protean expression of these roles, and he is nothing else. In this respect the novel exhibits one more instance of the Black Humorist's representation of a pluralistic world.

Here is no quest for lost innocence, no nostalgic lust for the return to leafy paradise and childhood comradeship. Black Humor has eschewed both the heroic and the tragic gestures in favor of the comic touched with *Angst* as appropriate for dealing with life in this century. An electronics culture is too faceless to elicit the heroic or tragic impulse. Only the transcendent safety valve of laughter adequately expresses one's scorn for the absurdity of it all and at the same time adequately refracts the monolithic facade of contemporary existence into recognizable—and endurable—human feelings again.

NOTES TO CHAPTER V

1. *The Hero of the Waverly Novels* (New Haven, 1963).

2. *Coleridge's Miscellaneous Criticism*, ed. Thomas M. Raysor (Cambridge, Mass., 1936), p. 335.

3. I am indebted in the following pages to Wylie Sypher's perceptive discussion, in *Loss of the Self in Modern Literature and Art* (New York, 1962), of the ironical contradiction of aims in the nineteenth century between the romantic assertion of the self and the liberal ideal of the greatest good for the greatest number.

4. There is, of course, the possibility that the ongoing intellectual and social revolution among the college-age generation is less a revolution in kind than in degree. The concern for the ecological crisis and for the survival of the human race may be their way of adjusting the old survival dogmas to new threats.

5. Roger Price, *The Great Roob Revolution* (New York, 1970), p. 125.

6. Jerzy Kosinski, "Dead Souls on Campus," *New York Times* (October 13, 1970), p. 43M.

7. For an acute evaluation of the sensibility of much modern art, see Saul Bellow, "Some Notes on Recent American Fiction," *Encounter*, XXI (1963), 22–29.

8. Richard Schechner, "Happenings," *Tulane Drama Review*, X (1965), 231.

122

9. "Allan Kaprow: A Happening," *ArtNews*, LXVI (1967), 71.

10. *Coleridge's Miscellaneous Criticism*, pp. 321–342.

11. "Spatial Form in Modern Literature," *The Sewanee Review*, LIII (1945), in three parts, 221–240, 433–456, 643–653; a condensed form is reprinted in *Criticism: The Foundations of Modern Literary Judgment*, ed. Mark Schorer, Josephine Miles, and Gordon McKenzie (New York, 1948), pp. 379–392.

12. *Ibid.*

13. Cf. Robert Goldwater, "Franz Kline: Darkness Visible," *ArtNews*, LXVI (1967), 39–43, 77.

14. Cf. John Perreault, "Krushenick's Blazing Blazons," *ArtNews*, LXVI (1967), 34–35, 72–73.

15. *The Sense of an Ending: Studies in the Theory of Fiction* (New York, 1967), p. 45.

16. Friedman, *Black Humor* (New York, 1965), p. viii.

17. *Ibid.*, p. x.

TEXT REFERENCES

John Barth
  The Sot-Weed Factor. New York: Doubleday and Company,
    1960; revised 1967.
  Giles Goat-Boy: or, The Revised New Syllabus. New York:
    Doubleday and Company, 1966.
  Lost in the Funhouse. New York: Doubleday and Company,
    1968.
Thomas Berger
  Little Big Man. New York: The Dial Press, 1964.
Henrich Böll
  Billiards at Half-past Nine. New York: McGraw, Hill & Com-
    pany, 1962.
  The Clown. New York: McGraw, Hill & Company, 1965.
    Translated by Leila Vennewitz.
Jorge Luis Borges
  Labyrinths. New York: New Directions, 1962. Edited by
    Donald A. Yates and James E. Irby and variously trans-
    lated.
  Other Inquisitions 1937–1952. Austin, Texas: University of
    Texas Press, 1965. Translated by Ruth L. C. Simms and
    Introduced by James E. Irby.
  The Book of Imaginary Beings. With Margaritta Guerro. New
    York: E. P. Dutton, 1969. Revised, Enlarged and Trans-
    lated by Norman Thomas di Giovanni in Collaboration
    with the Author.
Louis-Ferdinand Céline
  Journey to the End of the Night. New York: New Directions,
    1960. Translated by John H. P. Marks.
Leonard Cohen
  Beautiful Losers. New York: The Viking Press, 1966.

Robert Coover
The Universal Baseball Association, Inc. J. Henry Waugh, Prop. New York: Random House, 1968.
Bruce Jay Friedman
Stern. New York: Simon and Schuster, Inc., 1962.
A Mother's Kisses. New York: Simon and Schuster, Inc., 1964.
Günter Grass
The Tin Drum. New York: Random House, 1962. Translated by Ralph Manheim.
Joseph Heller
Catch-22. New York: Simon and Schuster, Inc., 1955.
Vladimir Nabokov
Lolita. New York: G. P. Putnam's Sons, 1966.
Thomas Pynchon
V. New York: J. B. Lippincott Company, 1963.
The Crying of Lot 49. New York: J. B. Lippincott Company, 1966.
Kurt Vonnegut, Jr.
Player Piano. New York: Holt, Rinehart and Winston, Inc., 1952.
The Sirens of Titan. New York: Dell Publishing Company, 1959.
Mother Night. New York: Harper and Row, 1961.
Cat's Cradle. New York: Holt, Rinehart and Winston, Inc., 1963.
God Bless You, Mr. Rosewater, or Pearls Before Swine. New York: Holt, Rinehart and Winston, Inc., 1965.
Slaughterhouse-Five: or the Children's Crusade. New York: The Delacorte Press, 1969.
Charles Wright
The Wig. New York: Farrar, Straus and Giroux, 1966.

TEXT REFERENCES

John Barth
   The Sot-Weed Factor. New York: Doubleday and Company,
   1960; revised 1967.

The plot of this story, patterned after the eighteenth-century
English novel with its mistaken identities, disguises, and complexities, almost defies summary. Ebenezer Cooke and his
twin sister Anna, born 1666, are tutored as children by Henry
Burlingame III. Eventually Eben's father decides to send him
to manage Malden, a sot-weed estate in Maryland. In London
preparatory to going to America, Eben falls in love with the
whore Joan Toast but decides that his innocence and poetical
prowess go hand in hand. He convinces Lord Baltimore that
he should be Maryland's Poet Laureate. On the way to Ply-
mouth Eben falls in with Burlingame, who tells of his birth in
the New World and of his unknown parentage. After sundry
adventures at sea brought on by Lord Baltimore's enemies
trying to prevent Eben from reaching Maryland, Eben arrives
in Dorset County, rescues an escaped Negro slave and an ill
Indian chief, inadvertently gives away Malden to a band of
political connivers bent on ruining the Province with pox and
opium as a means of overthrowing it, and is married to Joan
Toast, who followed him to the New World but through no
fault of her own has become so infected with pox and ruined
by opium that he does not recognize her. Disillusioned, Eben
writes a Hudibrastic satire of life in America. Crossing Chesa-
peake Bay he is captured by Indians and taken to their village.
There he meets the Negro and the Indian chief whom he had
succored and learns that Burlingame is the son of another
Indian chief and has two brothers, all three afflicted with
penises too small for sexual use, a genetic defect inherited

127

from their English grandfather Henry Burlingame who had accompanied Captain John Smith in explorations of the Bay. Eben's life is spared on condition that he bring Burlingame back to the Indian village. In search of his ex-tutor, Eben learns that his sister Anna has come to America and is living with one of Burlingame's Indian brothers, whom she loves for his similarity to Burlingame. At Malden he finds his father and Burlingame. A court of inquiry is held to determine who owns Malden. It is deeded to Joan Toast in exchange for lost papers of *The Privie Journal* of Sir Henry Burlingame, which along with *The Secret History* of Captain John Smith describes a Sacred Egg-plant stratagem that makes it possible for the Burlingames to copulate. Joan then deeds Malden over to her husband Eben when he consummates their marriage as atonement for all the wrongs his maintenance of innocence has perpetrated. Burlingame, using the egg-plant recipe, fathers a child on Anna and then disappears among the Indians with whom he shares half his blood. Eben and Anna live out their lives together in acknowledgement of the twinship which binds them. Thus, Eben finds in the New World not a new Eden but an extension of the chaos and the corruption of the Old World. And he learns that not in innocence but in the embrace of experience can man hope to come to terms with a world of immeasurable and meaningless multiplicity.

Giles Goat-Boy: or, The Revised New Syllabus. New York: Doubleday and Company, 1966.

Barth attempts in this book to distill all history and myth into one fable. Narrated allegorically as an academic novel, western civilization is West Campus, the eastern world East Campus, in cold-war rivalry with each other and fearful of a third campus riot. The power center of each campus is a giant computer, which programs all lethal actions and monitors all systems and operations. The hero George Goat-Boy combines the characteristics of the fertility-ritual-quest hero, as he re-enacts parodically the trials and success-failures of Oedipus and of Jesus. Of mysterious birth (found as a baby in the belly of WESCAC computer) and with a limp, he has been raised with goats by Professor Max Spielman, who has been expelled from New Tammany College in a quarrel over how to supplement the Oral examination after having helped to program WESCAC for EAT-weaponry and worked on the Cum Laude Project, perfecting the GILES (Grand-tutorial Ideal, Laboratory Eugenical Specimen). When George comes

128

of age and learns that he is a human, he announces himself as a candidate for Grand Tutor. He successfully performs a series of tests: scaling Main Gate (the Trial-by-Turnstile ceremony), getting through Scrapegoat Gate and matriculating, and solving a series of assignments that eventually disclose to him the truth of Commencement and of the enigmatic phrase connected with his birth, Pass All Fail All. He learns that his father is WESCAC programmed with GILES, an idealized blend of the sperm of all the students on West Campus. At every step his claim to be a Grand Tutor is challenged. The first two times he descends into the belly of WESCAC he is repudiated in favor of Professor Harold Bray, a rival contender. The third time he humbly accepts his commonality with all men and the indivisibility of pass-fail. He is led through WESCAC by Anastasia, granddaughter of the Chancellor of the University; hooded and coupled to her they push all the buttons on the console achieving a mystical moment of oneness, which leaves her impregnated with a second GILES. Although George does not reverse the AIM of WESCAC and thus lower the negative feeling between the two campuses, as had been his initial ambition, his teachings about selfless love lessen tension. For the next twelve years he lives quietly on West Campus recording directly into WESCAC's storage tapes a Revised New Syllabus of his teachings to replace the Founder's Scroll whose destruction he had been responsible for. For all its fabular effort to subsume all myth, the novel also clearly reflects the anxieties of the Cold-War Era of the 1950's and '60's and expresses the belief that only a miraculous reformulation of the view of man, of the world, and of transcendental thought, not unlike that which occurred two thousand years ago, is needed. As in *The Sot-Weed Factor*, not in innocence but in experience, in knowledge carnal and otherwise that reminds us anew of our infirmities as human beings, Barth suggests, lies our salvation.

Lost in the Funhouse. New York: Doubleday and Company, 1968.

Ostensibly a collection of thirteen stories, this book has a thematic unity and a narrative chronology. Concerned with the efforts of Ambrose to find his identity as an individual and as a writer, the stories progress from a mythic presentation of his conception through realistic presentations of moments in his boyhood to an ever-widening reach in time and in space toward correspondences with personal and bardic archetypes.

129

The stories are "Night-Sea Journey," "Ambrose His Mark,"
"Autobiography," "Water-Message," "Petition," "Lost in the
Funhouse," "Echo," "Two Meditations," "Title," "Glossola-
lia," "Life-Story," "Menelaiad," and "Anonymiad." The second story is a sensitively realized evocation of pre-Second
World War America narrating the humorous incident which
led to the naming of Ambrose. The fourth narrates Ambrose's
pre-adolescent awakening to sex and to the profound mystery
of life; and the sixth depicts his disintegrating personality under the twin assaults of adolescence and of artistic sensibility.
The next four stories deal with the author-narrator's problem
of finding a fictional voice. In the final two tales—which are
imaginative re-creations of the stories of Menelaus and of the
first anonymous bard who wrote prose narratives—Ambrose
and the author merge with their mythic progenitors, archetypes of man's quest to know who he is in relation emotionally
to whom he loves and imaginatively to all externality. The funhouse of the title story has obvious symbolic reference to the
world, which is less an endless organically varied extension in
time and space than a series of mirrored reflections of self that
extend in infinite regression back to first man and first artist.

Thomas Berger
Little Big Man. New York: The Dial Press, 1964.

Jack Crabb is a 110-year-old survivor of the Plains Indian
warfare, telling part of his story in 1952 to a well-to-do dilet-
tante collector of Americana. As an eleven-year-old he and
his older sister Caroline are captured by a band of Northern
Cheyenne who have massacred their wagon train in Nebraska
territory in 1852. His sister escapes, but he is adopted by the
chief Old Lodge Skins. In his first raid as a Cheyenne warrior
on a band of Crow Indians he saves the life of Younger Bear
(and incurs that worthy's enmity for life) and earns his name
Little Big Man. In 1857 during the first real engagement between the U.S. Army and the Cheyenne, in Kansas Territory,
he deserts to the whites, and is eventually adopted by the Rev-
erend Pendrake and taken to a town in western Missouri. He
has an adolescent crush on Mrs. Pendrake, but when he discovers that she is promiscuous, he lights out for Santa Fe,
drifts up to Denver when gold is discovered in Colorado,
operates a store in partnership with two other men, marries a
Swedish girl and has a son. Swindled by his partners, he flees
Denver in a stage coach, which is jumped by Cheyenne Indians
who capture his wife and son while he is getting help. He be-

comes a frontier bum and drunk, is rescued by his sister and becomes a mule skinner in 1865 helping in the building of the Union Pacific Railroad. In 1867 in an encounter with Cheyenne Indians he gets separated from the whites and finds himself back with the Indian band of his boyhood and with an Indian wife. They suffer with Black Kettle in the massacre on the Washita River. Crabb escapes but loses his Indian wife and child and vows he will kill General Custer, the victor. But it is winter and he is unable to keep up with the soldiers. For the next several years he roams the plains, surviving as a gambler and buffalo hunter. He is befriended by Will Bill Hickok and wins a shoot-out with him. In 1876 with the buffalo played out, he follows the army north into the Powder River country, becomes attached to Custer's Seventh Cavalry as a scout, and participates in the Battle of the Little Big Horn, where he is rescued by Younger Bear who thus evens his debt to Crabb for the action in the Crow raid years before. Crabb travels with Old Lodge Skins to the Black Hills. Both realize that the Indian way of life on the plains is finished. Old Lodge Skins climbs to the top of a mountain and dies. It is at this point in the narrative of his life that Crabb weakens and dies on 25 June 1953, the seventy-fifth anniversary of Custer's Last Fight; but his tale has sufficiently covered the crucial years of Indian warfare and settlement of the Plains in the second half of the nineteenth century to have recreated a portion of the myth of the Winning of the West.

Heinrich Böll
> *Billiards at Half-past Nine.* New York: McGraw, Hill & Company, 1962.

The time is 1958, the place a German city on the Rhine. Three generations of Faehmels—the founders of the line, Heinrich and Johanna; their son Robert; and his son and daughter, Joseph and Ruth—brood on the past, its few joys and triumphs and many heartaches, as they converge to celebrate Heinrich's eightieth birthday. Heinrich had arrived in town in 1907 a penniless unknown, had won in competition the contract to build St. Anthony's, which had made his reputation as an architect. His son Robert in the closing days of the Second World War blew it up in his capacity as a detonations expert. In the postwar era, Joseph rebuilds it. There is continuity here; but all three generations harbor bitter memories. Through two world wars they have scorned the blood lust of their German milieu. Heinrich passively greets it with irony, while his wife openly condemns it and ends finally in a mental asylum as a way of shutting it out of her sight. Robert is associated as a schoolboy with a group of Christian passivists, is beaten and forced to flee Germany for awhile, but is eventually pardoned, returns in time to serve in the German army, silently committed to blowing up things German in the name of German military need. His wife Edith, sister of Schrella with whom he fled Germany as a youth, is killed during the war. His children Joseph and Ruth remember with bitterness the years of their childhood when their grandmother would not give them enough to eat in her effort to atone for the evil being done by Germany. For Heinrich's birthday party, Johanna leaves the security of her asylum, Robert adopts a boy who reminds him of his wife and presents him to Heinrich as a new grandson, and Schrella returns from twenty-two years of exile and is received by Heinrich as another son. Family joy and love prevail but at a terrible price in human control, which demands that each seal off much of himself from the others, leading a private life of pain and anguish that is the submerged mass of the iceberg of his existence—the price each pays to continue to live with decency and sanity in Germany in a century when most people seem to have become mad dogs.

The Clown. New York: McGraw, Hill & Company, 1965. Translated by Leila Vennewitz

For five years Hans Schnier has barnstormed around West Germany as a comic mime with his Catholic mistress Marie Derkum, whom he had seduced but who refuses to marry him because of differences in religious belief. Increasingly distraught by religious scruples and influenced by a group of progressive Catholic friends, she deserts Hans to marry an important Catholic lay figure Heribert Züpfner. They go to Rome for their honeymoon and for the Pope's blessing. Hans, who is an innocent and irrevocably monogamous, is morally outraged by what he considers to be church-sanctioned adultery. He goes on a three-month drunk, begins to lose bookings, and finally hurts his leg in a performance. He returns to his and Marie's apartment in Bonn where he grew up, desperately broke and unable to earn a living at his art until his leg heals. In a long afternoon and evening of alternately self-pitying and acrid telephone calls, he tries to borrow money from acquaintances, friends, and family, most of whom he despises. He hangs up on his mother whom he detests because of her humorless commitment to principles that change with the occasion and because of her treatment of people as abstractions. Out of exaggerated sensibility for his father's feelings he lets that wealthy individual slip away without giving a penny. Even his younger brother Leo, a convert and a Catholic priest, offends him by a cautious subservience to the rules of his order, when Hans believes that Leo's Christian vocation should direct him to respond to a fellow human's appeal for help. Finally, in the evening, he decides to make up in white face, go to the Bonn railroad station, and play the guitar and sing for nickels and dimes. He knows such action is professional suicide, but the self-abasement suits his idea of himself and the scandalous behavior implies his criticism of the self-righteous Christians who have in one way or another refused his plea for help. Now they will have to walk past his outstretched hand.

Jorge Luis Borges
Labyrinths. New York: New Directions, 1962. Edited by Donald A. Yates and James E. Irby and variously translated.

This selection of Borges's writings, the first book-length publication in America, comes from *Ficciones* (1956), *El Aleph* (1957), *Discussión* (1957), *Otras Inquisiciones* (1960), and *El Hacedor* (1960). They include many of the short stories, essays, and parables on which his reputation is based: among the fictions, "Tlön, Uqbar, Orbis Tertius," "The Garden of Forking Paths," "Pierre Menard, Author of the *Quixote*," "The Circular Ruins," "The Library of Babel," "Funes the Memorious," "Death and the Compass," "The Immortal," "Averroes' Search," and "The Zahir"; among the essays, "The Wall and the Books," "The Fearful Sphere of Pascal," "Partial Magic in the *Quixote*," "Kafka and His Precursors," "Avatars of the Tortoise," and "A New Refutation of Time"; and among the parables, "A Problem," "Borges and I," and "Everything and Nothing." Borges is one of the pioneers and chief practitioners of a fiction that incorporates into its form the methods of the essay, the scholarly treatise, the exegesis, and the encyclopedic article. Such is the story "Pierre Menard," which constructs a bibliography of Menard's writings, with complete publishing history and footnoted memorabilia, and analyzes his major literary achievement. The ideas identified with Borges's fiction include a conception of the universe as a giant labyrinth without center, pattern, or end; a view of man as fallible, impermanent and shadowy, without inviolable selfness or persistent personality; and a

133

sense of the infinite vastness, the endless circularity, *regressus ad infinitum*, of time and of space and of human history. A profound skepticism tempered by a gentle whimsicality characterizes everything that Borges writes.

Other Inquisitions 1937–1952. Austin, Texas: University of Texas Press, 1965. Translated by Ruth L.C. Simms and Introduced by James E. Irby.

First published in 1952, these essays were Borges's second collection, with the title alluding to an early volume published in 1925, when he was twenty-five, and which he had come to look upon with disfavor as being the affected and dogmatic efforts of a young man. Repeatedly, the essays reveal similarities of theme and idea to be found in his stories, many of which masquerade as essays. There is the same skepticism, the same multiplicity of possibilities, the same conception of the universe as a dream and of man as a shadow, and the same admiration for the aestheticism of the human mind in its capacity to find correspondences in disparate things and actions and to create symmetries out of discordancies. Among the best-known of the essays are "The Wall and the Books," "Pascal's Sphere," "Partial Enchantments of the *Quixote*," "Kafka and His Precursors," "The Mirror of the Enigmas," "Avatars of the Tortoise," and "New Refutation of Time." There are also idiosyncratic appreciations of Coleridge, J.W. Dunne, P.H. Gosse, Quevedo, Hawthorne, Whitman, Valéry, Edward Fitz-Gerald, Wilde, Chesterton, H.G. Wells, Keats, Beckford, W.H. Hudson, and George Bernard Shaw. In all the essays the literary idiosyncrasies of Borges prevail: discursiveness, brevity, informality, antiquarianism, turn-of-the-century dandyism, comparativism, problematicability, heterogeneity, and "that imminence of a revelation that is not yet produced."

The Book of Imaginary Beings. With Margaritta Guerro. New York: E.P. Dutton, 1969. Revised, Enlarged and Translated by Norman Thomas di Giovanni in Collaboration with the Author.

An example of Borges's "useless and out-of-the-way erudition," this book is a compilation, alphabetically arranged, of imaginary animals, the fantastic zoo of mythology with its permutations and monstrosities. Borges's method is to summarize the characteristics of each animal, its traditional description and its permutations, as they are found for the most

134

part in the authorities of antiquity. The animals range from the A Bao A Qu to the Zaratan. In between, better-known ones cavort: Banshee, Behemoth, Centaur, Cerberus, Cheshire Cat and the Kilkenny Cats, innumerable Dragons, Golem, Harpies, Hippogriff, Kraken, Monkey of the Inkpot, Scylla, shaggy beast of La Ferté-Bernard, Troll, and Unicorn—altogether one hundred and twenty. The book is not without its serious side. As a witty and inventive reiteration of Borges's view of the world as one of dizzying chaos, infinitely permutative, the miscellany with its frank admission to the inexhaustibility of its subject offers us in these "strange creatures conceived through time and space by the human imagination" a companion to the variety of real animals conceived by nature. Thus, in his usual elliptical and allusive manner, Borges pays tribute to the synthesizing powers of the human mind and simultaneously to the poverty of its powers. The immensity of the task of combination is ultimately beyond the capacity of man's imagination. As Borges puts it, "Anyone looking into the pages of the present handbook will soon find out that the zoology of dreams is far poorer than the zoology of the Maker."

Louis-Ferdinand Céline
Journey to the End of the Night. New York: New Directions, 1960. Translated by John H.P. Marks.

Ferdinand Bardamu enlists in the French Army at the beginning of the First World War but quickly decides that war as conducted by his superiors is a stupidly obscene ritual of slaughter. He is wounded and during convalescence learns about women—an actress Musyne and an American nurse Lola. Both disillusion him about the fair sex. Eventually he is discharged as unfit for further military service. He goes to colonial French Africa where he observes another side of man's viciousness and stupidity. Assigned to a trading post in the interior, he is a failure, burns down the post, and in fleeing to the coast, falls ill of malaria. He is sold as a galley slave to a native ship master sailing to America. In New York he escapes, goes to Detroit, works in the Ford Motor plant, and meets and loves Molly. His restlessness prompts him, however, to return to France, even though he knows that running out on Molly is a foolish action. He becomes a medical doctor and settles down in a poor working class section of Paris to practice medicine. Here his education in the bestiality and

ignobility of man continues. He encounters his friend Robinson once again (Bardamu had first met him while in the army,
had run into him in Africa, and again in America), who tem-
porarily blinds himself trying to booby trap a rabbit hutch for
an avaricious couple bent on ridding themselves of an aged
mother. Robinson and the aged mother go to Toulouse to manage a catacomb. Bardamu meanwhile throws up his practice,
works in a theater for a while, and then gets a job as a doctor
in a small private mental asylum. Robinson meets a frivolous
girl, Madelon, who falls extravagantly in love with him. The
two push the old lady down stairs and kill her. Loath to be
loved, Robinson flees to Bardamu, who gets him a job at the
asylum. Madelon shows up hurling accusations of homosexuality at the two men. On an all day excursion to a fair with
Madelon an effort is made to pacify her but she gets progres-
sively abusive and finally shoots Robinson. After laying out
his corpse, Bardamu goes off to a bar on the canal brooding
that all men are doomed to die, which epitomizes the bleak,
often savage, tone of the novel. In Bardamu's eyes, man is a
dying sack of ordure and life is a cheat—and his adventures
detailed in the novel confirm this view.

Leonard Cohen
Beautiful Losers. New York: The Viking Press, 1966.

In the first section, the narrator is Larry, a folklorist and
authority on American Indians, living in a treehouse five years
after the death of his friend and homosexual lover F. Earlier,
Larry's Indian wife Edith had committed suicide and Larry
had learned from F. that he and she had been lovers, indeed,
had been in league to create in Larry a New Man, one who is
not restricted to genital eroticism but is erotogenous over the
total surface of his body. To this end F. devises three tests
designed to remake Larry, who fails them all. Similarly, Edith
becomes frigid and F. has to bring a Danish Vibrator to her
aid. Among his bits of advice, F. recommends that Larry
copulate with a saint. Larry obliges by trying to bring off the
feat imaginatively with a seventeenth-century Iroquois named
Catherine Tekakwitha, the first Indian virgin saint. The second
section is a long letter by F. written in a hospital. He dies in a
padded cell, his brain rotted from venereal disease. Ironically,
it is F. who gives us both the history of Catherine Tekakwitha's last days of self-flagellated denial of the body and of
Edith's final sexual martyrdom with the vibrator. In effect,
both women are victims of an ideal, one unitive and spiritual,

the other pluralistic and corporeal. The third section depicts Larry's return to Montreal in apocalyptic terms. A stinking pile of rags and ghostliness, he disintegrates and then reassembles himself by way of identification with celluloid cinema images. F. and Larry's sexual nonconformity is one level of a total rebellion against the establishment. Spiritually they reject all externally imposed systems of thought. Politically they reject British Canada's hegemony over French speaking Quebec. Historically they reject the Catholic Church's institutionalized version of the salvation of North America. And geopolitically they deplore Canada's artistic and intellectual isolation. The degree to which they realize their revolt in viable terms remains a moot question to be answered by each reader.

Robert Coover
The Universal Baseball Association, Inc. J. Henry Waugh, Prop. New York: Random House, 1968.

Henry Waugh is a boozy fifty-six year old bachelor bookkeeper with a flair for statistics and percentages. He has devised a three-dice baseball game, which consists of eight teams with a complete roster of players each with his individual history. In addition he records the history of each season of play. He is currently in the midst of the fifty-sixth season. Rookie Damon Rutherford of the Pioneers, son of the great Brock Rutherford, pitches a no-hitter against the Knickerbockers. Two games later, pitching again, Damon is killed by a bean ball pitched by Jock Casey of the Knickerbockers. Absorbed by the baseball world he is creating, Waugh does badly in his accountant's job and eventually is fired. Obsessed with Damon's death, he arranges the dice so that Jock Casey is killed by a line drive; then in a frenzy of play he finishes that season and writes a history of the first fifty-six years of the Association disclosing a pattern not of perfection but of process toward an ever more moral and philosophical concern with the nature of man and society. In the eighth and final chapter of the novel Waugh has disappeared but the Association continues. It is the 157th season. The fates of Damon Rutherford and of Jock Casey have been conflated into one action, reenacted annually by the players. Although not certain of the ontological revelations of this pattern of history, most players accept the Caseyite view of the universe, which attempts to bring order out of chaos. The baseball game is clearly being manipulated by Coover to correspond to the Judeo-Christian story of man, with J. Henry Waugh (JHWH, Yahweh) as God; Damon, the ritual god of nature; Jock Casey, Jesus Christ; Barney Bancroft who writes the first history of the Association (the Old Testament), a representative of the Hebrew Sanhedrin; and Patrick Monday who gives the Association a new beginning, St. Paul. Thus originate the myths, says Coover, by which man sustains his need to have a history, his need to arrange a random chain of accidents into a ritualistic and meaningful sequence.

Bruce Jay Friedman
  Stern. New York: Simon and Schuster, Inc., 1962.

Stern is an insecure urban Jew who has moved with his wife and child to the suburbs. There he is surrounded by anti-semitic neighbors. His wife is either pushed by an Italian-American kike-hater or slips and falls, accidentally displaying herself. Brooding over the real or fancied insult to his wife, Stern tries to summon courage to demand an apology from the "kike-man"; but fantasies of neighborhood pogroms and of violence done to his family terrorize him and prevent his confronting the man. The upshot of his obsession with this failure of his manhood (and with his fears of his wife's infidelities) is an ulcer. He goes to a rest home, where he plays baseball, becomes friends with two young patients with whom he sneaks off the grounds at night for a beer and sexual foolery with one boy's Puerto Rican girlfriend, and finally after some weeks returns home with the pain from the ulcer gone. But his anxiety about the kike-hating neighbor continues. He has a minor nervous breakdown. Eventually he gains some perspective on the episode, seeing it for what it was: "an ignorant remark, a harmless shove, no one really hurt, much time elapsed, so what." This new calm lasts a short while. Then one night at the dinner table, he begins to breathe hard. He goes outside to get his breath and finds himself at the kike-man's house inviting him outside for a fight. Each man throws one punch, Stern's ineffectual, the kike-man's connecting with Stern's ear. Home again, Stern begins to shake with fear of the man all over again. He puts his arms around his wife and son in a loving protective gesture and ends holding on to them in turn. Psychosexually, Stern both envies and deplores the kike hater's prowess. As the ravaged Jew longing for acceptance into the mainstream of American culture, he equates the kike hater's masculinity with things American. Friedman thus

138

expands the Jewish theme with its potential violence to include the larger social context of the civil violence every citizen faces in mid-century America.

A Mother's Kisses. New York: Simon and Schuster, Inc., 1964.

Joseph is a seventeen-year-old Brooklyn boy worrying about getting accepted into a college; yet inexplicably he applies to only two, Bates College which is out of town and Columbia University. He is also a young man ambivalently trying to break free of a domineering mother. Inevitably, Bates rejects his application. To get his mind off his problem and to keep him from mooning about the house, his mother arranges for him to work as a waiter at a summer camp. Joseph finds to his chagrin that he is a camper waiter, bunking with fourteen-year-olds and forced to observe the rules governing them, which includes restrictions against late hours. The latter aborts his flings at romance with a fast French girl; and his own fears inhibit him with an Austrian girl who has a history of mental illness. Then, he learns that Columbia has turned him down. In self-pity he spiritlessly rifles the lockers of some of the waiters, is caught, and is brought back to New York City by his mother, who nurses an infection in his arm. Eventually she engineers his acceptance by Kansas Land Grant Agricultural and accompanies him to the overpopulated college town to see that he finds a place to live. They move into a hotel and Joseph begins to attend classes. Meg, his mother, stays on and on to oversee as usual Joseph's eating, laundry, etc., neither happy with the presence of the other there but neither willing to cut himself free. They half-heartedly look for living quarters for Joseph, who tentatively strikes up friendships with fellow students and timidly approaches girls at a neighboring girl's college. In a night of angry retorts, Joseph throws up to his mother all the years in which she has dragged him about in her female world of girdles, bras, and hairdressers. Finally, she accepts the idea that Joseph will not leave college and return with her to NYC. Joseph responds to her departure with mixed feelings but he lets her go. Although the vitality of Friedman's portrait of Meg as a beleaguered Jewish mother threatens the thematic balance of the novel, Friedman's focus in the narrative is on Joseph's Oedipal relationship with his mother and on his adolescent forays into the unknown world of girls. In development of the latter theme, the novel explores the mystik of love and sex as encountered by an adolescent in a mid-century America which derives its model, in part, from Hollywood and the cinema.

Günter Grass
The Tin Drum. New York: Random House, 1962. Translated by Ralph Manheim.

It is 1953. Oskar Matzerath sits in his hospital bed (he is there as a mental patient and convicted murderer—of a crime he has not committed) and alternately writes and drums on his child's tin drum the story of his life, starting with his Kashubian Polish grandparents at the beginning of the century. In 1923 his mother marries Alfred Matzerath, a Rhinelander, in Danzig. They buy a grocery store and settle down to the life of petit bourgeois shopkeepers. Oskar is born the same year. At the age of three he decides not to grow anymore, as a way of evading his parents' desire to put him eventually behind the grocery counter. Instead he becomes a drummer on a succession of child's toy drums. His parents' best friend is Oskar's mother's cousin and lover, Jan Bronski. In 1937 or 1938 Oskar's mother wearies of her sexual triangle and of Oskar's perpetual childhood, gorges herself on fish, sickens, and dies. Uncertain of which of the two men—Bronski or Matzerath—is his father, Oskar in the war years that follow is responsible for both their deaths. He also begets a child on Maria Truczinki, his father's second wife. At the end of the Second World War and following Alfred Matzerath's burial, he gives up drumming, and grows to four feet, which twists his body in a hump on his back. He, Maria, and their son Kurt migrate to West Germany, settling in Düsseldorf, where Kurt, having earlier rejected Oskar's efforts to make a drummer out of him, deals in the Black Market with the instincts of a shopkeeper. Disgustedly, Oskar apprentices himself to a cutter of tombstones. He takes up drumming again, becomes a famous musician, and buys Maria a delicatessen store. But he is haunted, like most Germans, by guilty memories, which he alternately drums to forget or to recall from the past. Increasingly his conscience terrifies him, appearing in the form of a Black Witch (linked in his mind with a children's game)—who contrasts to the many motherly women and white clad nurses whom he has been drawn to during his thirty years of life. He allows himself to be prosecuted for the murder of a nurse he had loved at a distance, and thereby gains the antiseptic safety of the mental hospital in which he writes his life story. Oskar and his toy tin drum represent Germany; and in Oskar's willful stunting of his growth, in his alternating attraction to Goethe and Rasputin, in his and Maria's erotic infatuation with fizz powder, in his rejection of his fathers, in his postwar successes, and in his intermittent remorse, Grass means to dramatize the Germany of this century with its turning aside from its traditional frugal and serious ways to chase after exotic and profane lures.

Joseph Heller
Catch-22. New York: Simon and Schuster, Inc., 1955.

It is the Second World War, with a U.S. bomber squadron on an island in the Mediterranean near Elba. Captain Yossarian is a bombardier who has decided after more than forty missions that people are trying to kill him. The moment of enlightenment for him occurs when a young gunner named Snowden dies in his arms, disemboweled by flak. From then on it becomes Yossarian's mission to stay alive until he has completed his required number of missions. The trouble is that Colonel Cathcart in an effort to ingratiate himself with his superiors keeps upping the missions needed for rotation home until it reaches over seventy. At war with the military bureaucracy rather than with the Germans, Yossarian dumps his bombs willy-nilly and gets himself sent to the base hospital with undiagnosable ailments as often as possible. But nothing eventually prevents his flying seventy-one missions. One by one most of his old flying buddies die. Finally, Yossarian decides to refuse to fly anymore. He goes AWOL but is picked up by M.P.'s and returned to the base. Because he is considered a hero for inadvertently flying his squadron around twice over the bomb target at Ferrara before knocking it out, Colonels Cathcart and Korn make a deal to send him home for public-relations purposes. His alternative is a court martial. Yossarian agrees at first to this deal. Leaving the Colonels' offices he is stabbed by his friend Nately's whore, who holds Yossarian responsible for Nately's death because Yossarian had brought her the bad news. In the hospital Yossarian decides not to play ball with the colonels but to desert and make his way to Sweden, as had his tentmate Orr. In his resistance to a system which is trying to get him killed, Yossarian finds himself in opposition to the opportunism and bureaucratic officiousness of Colonel Cathcart, of Lieutenant Milo Minderbinder, the mess officer who runs an international cartel of food imports and exports, which ignores national boundaries

141

and alliances and humanitarian considerations, of General Sheisskopf whose model of reality is a parade of soldiers, and of ex-P.F.C. Wintergreen, a mail clerk through whom all communications (and hence all official orders and preferments) are channeled. Ultimately, then, the object of satire is prophetically as much the mindless and faceless bureaucratic institutions of post war American society as the lunacy of the Second World War.

Vladimir Nabokov
Lolita. New York: G.P. Putnam's Sons, 1966.

Humbert Humbert, a fortyish French-speaking Swiss, is in jail for the murder of Clare Quilty. While awaiting trial, he composes a confessional memoir designed as an ingratiating defense of his actions to the jury. His life is a tale of obsessive love of nymphets, girls between nine and fourteen, not yet women but already exuding a sexual sense of self. His perversion has its start at thirteen when a passionate romance with a child his age is never consummated. For the next thirty years he seeks that girl in the image of every nymphet he meets. In his mid-thirties he comes to America, meets the nymphet Lolita, daughter of Charlotte his landlady, and marries the mother to be near the daughter. Charlotte learns of Humbert's perverse desire, but before she can do anything about it, she is run down by a car which she does not see in her blind rage. After burying her, Humbert picks up Lolita at summer camp bent on enjoying his fill of her imaginatively; but at the end of their first night in a motel, he learns of her sexual adventures at camp and ends being willingly seduced by her. For the next several years he subjects Lolita to a brutal existence, exacting monstrous sexual demands of her daily and threatening her with an orphanage and worse should she disclose their relationship. They make two cross country tours of America. During the second, she conspires with Quilty, a pervert even more gross than Humbert, whom she met while acting in one of his plays in high school, to spirit her away. About three years later Humbert has a letter from Lolita announcing that she is married, is expecting, and needs money to finance her and her husband's way to Alaska where he has a job awaiting him. Humbert, who knows now that he loves the woman Lolita, rather than the idealized image of a nymphet who exists nowhere but in his mind's eye, seeks her out, begs her to no avail to return to him, and finally gives her the money inherited at her mother's death. He has lost Lolita forever but

142

he learns from her that she had run off with Quilty. Humbert promptly kills him and is apprehended by the police. In the course of writing his memoir, Humbert comes to realize the crime he has perpetrated against Lolita, essentially robbing her of her childhood and scarring her emotionally for life. He advises the jury that they should give him at least thirty-five years for rape, and dismiss the rest of the charges. He dies of a heart attack before he comes to trial and Lolita dies in childbirth. At the end all that remains as testimony of his passion is his memoir, whose artistic rendering gives a permanence to his love that he never realized in actuality.

Thomas Pynchon
V. New York: J.B. Lippincott Company, 1963.

Two narratives run parallel, occasionally intersecting, lines in this novel, and like the Elizabethan play, one is low comedy, the other high drama. Benny Profane, schlemiel, embodies in his lack of direction in life the entropic theme that also underlies the view of history developed in the novel. With The Whole Sick Crew, a loose group of NYC dissidents, freakish artists, and way-out entertainment world figures, Benny drifts from party to party, into occasional jobs engineered by friends or by Rachel Owlglass, the girl he loves, and finally to Malta with Herbert Stencil, where he is last seen running down a street of Valletta with a girl he has picked up, an action similar to and equally pointless as his escapade in Norfolk, Virginia, in the scene opening the novel almost a year previously. Profane has not grown in knowledge or moral awareness. He continues to "run down", a socio-biological confirmation of the Second Law of Thermodynamics, only slightly more alive than the robots he oversees as an employee of Anthroresearch Associates. Contrariwise, Stencil's life is dedicated, no more meaningfully perhaps, to reconstructing the history of a shadowy woman known only by the letter V., whose fate crisscrosses that of his father, an undercover agent for the British Foreign Office at the turn of the century. Out of a few mementoes inherited from his father and a vast network of places and people tied together by the coincidences of his father's presence and of the letter V. appearing in proper names, Stencil weaves a fantasy of fact and conjecture into a sequence of history stretching from 1899 to the post-Second-World-War years with the emphasis on the recurrence of crisis in which mysterious evil forces are bent on upsetting the good status quo. The girl V. metamorphoses from Victoria Wren to Vera

Monroving to Veronica Manganese, appearing in Cairo in 1899 coincident with the Fashoda Incident, in Florence, Italy, later that year in the midst of a minor Venezuelan rebellion, in Warmbad, German South West Africa in 1922 during a native uprising, and in Valletta, Malta, in 1919, at the height of the agitation for home rule, disappearing finally during an air raid bombing of Valletta in 1940. At her death, as the Bad Priest, she is discovered to have methodically replaced parts of her body with metal, thus "disappearing" in another literal sense, as well as embodying the man-become-machine theme of the novel. The novel is a vast parodic warehouse of literary styles and of the cataclysmic state of mind of twentieth-century man. In this frame of reference, Benny Profane functions as the modern anti-quest hero. Herbert Stencil contrariwise figures as the traditional quest hero, but new modeled in the contemporary mode of a Quixote aware that his search is an adventure of the mind, an intellectual gesture of order flung out against the illogic and patternlessness of events.

The Crying of Lot 49. New York: J.B. Lippincott Company. 1966.

The title alludes to the auctioning of a batch of stamps, all forgeries, part of the estate of Pierce Inverarity, a California real estate mogul. Recently dead, Inverarity has named Oedipa Maas co-executor of his will. In the course of her performing these duties she becomes privy to a complex of circumstantial facts that point to an underground world of information flow begun in the sixteenth century by one Tristero y Calavera, who began an organization in opposition to the postal monopoly of Thurn and Taxis. The Tristero group, whose adversary role took on religious and political associations over the centuries, manifesting itself in subversive resistance to the Holy Roman Empire, to the Bourbon reign in France, and to the Pony Express in America, created its own postal stamps by clever alterations of the official stamps (Inverarity's collection of forgeries are instances of these) and its own secret motto and channels of communication (in California this takes the form of using urban W.A.S.T.E. containers with the subversive meaning We Await Silent Tristero's Empire). Oedipa Maas discovers references to Tristero, among other places, in variant lines of a seventeenth-century Revenge Play, in the import-export machinations of the Cosa Nostra, in the interoffice delivery system in Inverarity's Yoyodyne Corporation. Slowly, before her disbelieving eyes, the Tristero movement emerges as a vast underground force of reactive energy, functioning as a revolutionary threat to oppressive establishments of debilitating order and as a replenishment of energy in the world dissipated according to the law of entropy. All the references to Tristero Oedipa stumbles on can be traced back to the Inverarity estate. The novel ends with her sitting in an auction room awaiting the crying of lot 49 (the bogus Tristero stamps), and wondering if she is hallucinating, is suffering from paranoia, is the victim of a colossal prank by Inverarity, or has had disclosed to her a compensatory force in the universe working to offset the effect of entropy.

Kurt Vonnegut, Jr.
   Player Piano. New York: Holt, Rinehart and Winston, Inc., 1952.

The time is the not too distant future; the place is Ilium, New York. Following a great war, America has become almost totally automated. Society is divided into an elite class of engineers and systems managers, and into the proletarian classes of the military and the Reconstruction and Reclamation Corps (the "Reeks and Wrecks"). Most of the population fits into the latter categories. Unable to compete economically with machines, they are sustained by a paternalistic welfare system. Paul Proteus is manager of the Ilium Works. His best friend is Ed. Finnerty, a brilliant engineer who has just quit the prestigious National Industrial Planning Board in repudiation of a social hierarchy that measures men against machines. Paul similarly finds his managerial position increasingly indefensible, his life circumscribed by the rules of the system, and his superiors insensitive louts. Yet he is slated for promotion to the management of the Pittsburgh Works, contingent on his betraying Finnerty, who has become part of an underground rebellion against the managerial class. Paul decides to resign; but he procrastinates, attending the annual inspirational gathering of the country's top management personnel at the Meadows. There he is ordered by the National Director to infiltrate the rebellious organization now known as the Ghost Shirts after the religious movement of the American Indians in the 1890's. At a meeting of the leaders of the Society, whose aim is to destroy the machines and to restore to man his dignity and his usefulness, Paul allows himself to be heralded as the Messiah of the movement. Captured, he is put on trial for conspiracy and sabotage. During the proceedings a riot breaks out, Paul is rescued, and the revolution is begun. Except for success in Ilium and several other cities, the rebellion is quickly contained by the government. When Proteus and Finnerty see skilled mechanics repairing the smashed machines, they realize that their desire to demonstrate that man can live happily with virtually no machines is doomed by man's pride in his ability to make things. They surrender to the authorities, disillusioned by the sight of men they had sought to help eagerly recreating the same old technological nightmare.

The Sirens of Titan. New York: Dell Publishing Company, 1959.

Malachi Constant is one of the richest financiers in America. He is also an unsavory Hollywood denizen, a man lacking in values and sense of style. His luck as a speculator fizzles out, however, and he goes broke. Running from creditors he goes to Mars as a lieutenant colonel in its army. En route he rapes Beatrice Rumfoord, wife of Newport scion Winston Niles Rumfoord. On Mars he is demoted to private, renamed Unk, and repeatedly hospitalized to have his memory wiped out and his mind programmed to make him function as a robot-like soldier. Beatrice after bearing Malachi's son Chrono also undergoes the same operations. But both struggle to remember, to create a history. After eight years, the pitifully inadequate Martian army invades Earth. All but a handful perish. Among the survivors are Beatrice and Chrono. Unk's invasion space ship takes him to Mercury instead of Earth, and only after three years is he able to escape. When he arrives on Earth he discovers that the Martian invaders have been proclaimed martyrs and a new religion has arisen known as the Church of God the Utterly Indifferent, which sees life as a series of accidents, of good and bad luck. His miraculous appearance as the Weary Space Wanderer has been prophesied and he is hailed as some kind of savior. Shortly after being reunited with his son and mate however, the populace turns against him. Dutifully he boards a space ship for Titan, the greatest moon of Saturn, accompanied by Beatrice and Chrono. There they encounter Salo, a Tralfamadorian carrying a single-word-message of "Greeting" from one rim of the universe to the other. He began his trip almost 500,000 years ago. In 203,117 B.C. he was forced down on Titan by mechanical difficulties and has been waiting for the delivery of a replacement part ever since. It is in the pocket of Chrono, a good-luck piece he picked up on Mars. Also on Titan is Winston Niles Rumfoord, who had run his private space ship years before into an uncharted chrono-synclastic infundibulum (or time-space warp) between Mars and Earth, which scattered him in spiral pulsations through the solar system, allowing him to materialize only when a heavenly body intercepts his spirals. The spirals of Rumfoord and Titan coincide exactly; hence he is permanently materialized there as contrasted to his materialization on Earth every fifty-nine days. All that has happened to Unk, Beatrice, and the Martian-Earthlings in the past twenty odd years was maneuvered by Rumfoord, who in turn was manipulated by Tralfamadorians, who have also been responsible for every event on Earth since the beginning of man—all directed toward delivery of the replacement part to Salo. Thus, the entire narrative is illustrative of the opening remarks that man's exploration of space merely extends the nightmare of meaninglessness ever outward without end.

Mother Night. New York: Harper and Row, 1961.

Howard W. Campbell, Jr., is American born, but he grew up, married, and elected to stay in Germany between the Wars. He becomes a playwright and in 1938 is recruited as an American agent. Throughout the Second World War he broadcasts vicious diatribes against the Allies, which carry coded information. Captured at the end of the war, he is quietly released but without acknowledgement from the U.S. Government of the part he has played and allowed to return to New York City where he lives as a recluse. In 1960 his identity is disclosed by a neighbor with whom Campbell has become friendly, but who is a Russian agent with a plan to spirit Campbell to Russia and to display him as a Fascist protected by the American government. Campbell's younger sister-in-law is recruited to impersonate his dead wife returned from years of internment in Russia and East Germany. She contacts Dr. L.J.D. Jones, publisher of the American Fascist paper *The White Christian Minuteman*, who takes her to Campbell. He is warned in time by the anonymous American agent who had recruited him in Germany; but the world-wide hue and cry for revenge reaches what has been his dead heart and mind and he turns himself over to the Israeli government to be tried for war crimes. The day before his trial Campbell receives a letter from the American agent identifying himself and offering to affirm under oath Campbell's role as spy during the war. By this time, though, Campbell is convinced that he performed

147

so well as a Nazi because his inner person had found the role irresistible and because he had allowed his feelings and moral sense of right and wrong to be anesthetized against evil. In serving evil openly, and good secretly, he became what he pretended to be. For this crime against himself he decides to hang himself rather than wait for the Israeli to put him on trial.

Cat's Cradle. New York: Holt, Rinehart and Winston, Inc., 1963.

This book is about the nature of knowledge. Felix Hoenikker, Nobel Prize physicist and one of the chief creators of the atom bomb, approached the unlocking of the secrets of the universe all his life as if it were child's play. In such a spirit he also discovered how to rearrange the molecules of water so that they locked into ice-like crystals called ice-nine; he died shortly after making a batch in the kitchen sink. Only his three children know of this. Each keeps a sliver of it. Frank Hoenikker uses his to get himself a job as Minister of Science and Progress in the Caribbean island Republic of San Lorenzo. Jonah, the narrator, a free-lance writer who has been researching the life of Hoenikker preparatory to doing a book on the first atomic bomb, is assigned by a magazine to do a story on Julian Castle, an American millionaire medical missionary on San Lorenzo. Jonah learns that all the islanders are Bokononists, an outlawed religion of a Tobagoan Black named Johnson. Bokononism argues in Calypso limericks that all true things are shameless lies and that the way to reach the soul of another is to rub the soles of his feet with one's own. Jonah also falls in love with Mona Aamons Monzano, the beautiful adopted mulatto daughter of "Papa" Monzano, the mortally ill ruler of the island. Jonah accepts Frank Hoenikker's offer to be the next President of San Lorenzo, since marriage to Mona goes with the position. An air show is scheduled in celebration of an island holiday. During the festivities, Papa Monzano, wracked with pain from cancer, commits suicide by swallowing a sliver of ice-nine he had gotten from Frank Hoenikker. He immediately freezes stiff as a board. One of the planes in the air show crashes into the cliff on which the president's castle sits, causing a rock slide that undermines the castle walls. As part of the building crumbles into the sea, the room in which Papa Monzano's corpse lies is exposed, tilts, and Papa Monzano drops into the ocean, starting an ice-nine reaction. In a week the world is locked up ice-tight. Jonah and Mona among others survive the cosmic tornadoes in an oubliette. During the next six months he writes a history of human stupidity; then, as Mona and other survivors had done earlier, he commits suicide by touching tongue to the blue-white frost covering everything rather than continue to live in the now universe of death. So much for belief that the advance of knowledge is always good.

God Bless You, Mr. Rosewater, or Pearls Before Swine. New York: Holt, Rinehart and Winston, Inc., 1965.

Eliot Rosewater is fortyish and president of the Rosewater Foundation, the repository of the fourteenth largest family fortune in America. He is also a drunk, a volunteer fireman enthusiast, a science fiction buff, an impotent neurotic, and a modern Good Samaritan. Afflicted with guilt feelings for having accidentally killed his mother in a boating incident and three unarmed German firemen during the Second World War and for having so much wealth, he retires to the town and county of Rosewater, Indiana, where most of the people are either employed, or have been bilked, by the Rosewater Corporation which concentrates on realizing profits and thus increasing the size of the Rosewater Foundation. For five years he entertains only the local morons, perverts, starvelings, and unemployed. Then his wife Sylvia suffers a nervous collapse; after her recovery she flees to France, has a relapse, and begins divorce proceedings. Eliot moves into an empty dentist's office (which he hardly ever leaves) over a lunch room and liquor store and continues to dispense love and largesse indiscriminately to the town's misfits, advertising his phone number randomly in phone booths and in the back windows of cars and trucks of volunteer firemen. Accused by his father Senator Lister of smashing every hope and ideal he had for Eliot and of ruining the life and health of a woman whose only fault is loving him, Eliot has a nervous breakdown accompanied by total amnesia of the years spent in Rosewater, Indiana. Meanwhile, Eliot's cousin Fred, who lives in Rhode Island, learns that he is descended from the impoverished brother of Eliot's great-grandfather, and that he is next in line should Eliot die or be declared insane without issue. During the year Eliot spends in a sanitorium, Fred sues to have him declared insane. Just before the court case is to be convened, Eliot recovers from his amnesia to hear his father and Kilgore Trout, a science fiction writer whom Eliot admires, declaring that his social experiment in Rosewater County was the most important of our time, since it attempted to come to grips with the problem of how to love people who have become socially useless. Learning of Fred's law suit and of fifty-seven paternity cases pending against him, Eliot writes a check for one hundred thousand dollars for Fred and orders the legal counsel of the Foundation to draw up papers acknowledging that every child in Rosewater County said to be his is his. Thus, with one stroke of the pen, Eliot insures continuation of his philanthropy and perpetuation of the Rosewater Foundation.

Slaughterhouse-Five: or the Children's Crusade. New York: The Delacorte Press, 1969.

Billy Pilgrim has come unstuck in time. On the night of his daughter's wedding in 1967 he is kidnapped by Tralfamadorians and taken to their planet where he is placed on display in a zoo and mated with an American pornomovie queen Montana Wildhack. The Tralfamadorians teach him that time as earthlings know it is fictive; all past and all future moments exist in an everlasting now. Billy is taught to travel backward and forward in his life, that is to "remember" the past and the future. The narrative sequence conforms to this simultaneity of events, rather than to conventional linear chronology. Four episodes in Billy's life—his boyhood, his Second World War experiences, his post war years as a family man and prosperous optometrist in Ilium, New York, and his abduction by the Tralfamadorians—are presented in short disjunctive flashbacks and flashforwards. The most important of these follow his contretemps as a soldier. As a replacement in an infantry regiment caught in the Battle of the Bulge, he is captured without having fired a shot, indeed without having been issued helmet and combat boots. He is sent to Dresden as a prisoner of war, survives the 1945 fire-bombing of the city by being quartered in a cement-block slaughterhouse with a meat locker under it. Mustered out after the war, he marries the daughter of the owner of the Ilium School of Optometry, is set up in business by his father-in-law, has two children, and prospers. In 1968 he attends a convention of optometrists in Montreal. The plane carrying him crashes, killing everyone but him. His wife dies of carbon monoxide poisoning en route to the hospital where he is recovering. Out of the hospital, Billy suddenly goes to New York City and on an all-night radio program describes his kidnapping by Tralfamadorians as prelude to his message that death is appearance and time illusory; but he is considered to be a crackpot. Eventually, Billy claims, he will die in 1976, following the hydrogen bombing of Chicago by

150

the Chinese, assassinated while attending a meeting on flying saucers and the true nature of time. Ostensibly an attack on war (in a long first chapter, the author describes his survival of the 1945 fire-bombing of Dresden) the narrative broadens its reference to include every conceivable way in which man inevitably meets death, thus reducing war to something as common as eating and sleeping, a natural process of life and hence not tragic but a part of the comic odyssey of man.

Charles Wright
The Wig. New York: Farrar, Straus and Giroux, 1966.

An American Negro living in an airless vermined rooming house in Harlem, and feeling trapped socially and economically, Lester Jefferson optimistically decides that he will get a share of the Great Society promised all Americans. Using Silky Smooth Hair Relaxer, he straightens and yellows his hair. With his friend Little Jimmie, a has-been movie star whose image has failed to keep pace with the new militant Black profile, Lester tries to break into the recording business with a music routine; but his ambition outstrips his skills. A living repudiation of white America's stereotype of the Negro, he cannot even carry a tune. He does better with a 125th Street Black prostitute known as The Deb, who takes him to be a foreigner because of his hair. But Lester is not satisfied to have her under false pretenses; he acts the mean Black lover and she walks out on him, bitter at learning that he is a Nigger. Sold on the American Dream of working one's way up the ladder of success, Lester takes a job impersonating a chicken on the streets of New York City to advertise The King of Southern Fried Chicken. Depressed by the loss of The Deb, he puts himself in the hands of Mr. Fishback, the funeral director, who cuts off his hair and cauterizes his penis, unmasking Lester to disclose him once again as the meek unvirile American Negro. As a Black version of the Horatio Alger hero, Lester presents us with a series of roles he plays in his effort to be what he thinks the white man wants him to be, what the Black man conceives him to be, and what each race fobs off on the other as a stereotype. Sardonically, the novel suggests that Lester—like another victim of the American Dream, Lemuel Pitkin in Nathanael West's *A Cool Million*—has no identity separate from what he pretends to be.

Index

Albee, Edward, 3
Alienation, Characters, 8–9
Amis, Kingsley, 87
Appel, Alfred, 22
Arschwager, Richard, 54–55
Atemporality, see Black Humor
Auden, W. H.

Auden, W. H., 93

Baker, Elliot: *A Fine Madness*, 99
Barth, John, 3, 5, 6–7, 21–22, 51, 72,
  89; *The End of the Road*, 29; exhaustion of guises of reality, 23,
  29–40; *The Floating Opera*, 10,
  17, 29; *Giles Goat-Boy*, 29–32, 40,
  44, 105, 128–129; identity of self,
  33–40; *Lost in the Funhouse*, 32–
  40, 44, 129–130; metaphysics of
  multiplicity, ix; *The Sot-Weed Factor*, x, 11, 13, 17–18, 25, 27, 29–
  31, 44, 87–88, 94, 105, 127–128;
  regressus in infinitum, 36–40
Baudelaire, Charles: *Le Fleur du
  Mal*, 33
Beckett, Samuel, 6, 52
Bellow, Saul, 87
Bennett, Arnold, 87
Berger, Thomas, 89; *Crazy in Berlin*,
  72; *Little Big Man*, 27, 72–77,
  130–131; parody, ix, 72–77; *Reinhart in Love*, 72
Black Humor, atemporality, 103–
  108; comic apocalypse, 78–82; conformist hero, 91–101, 109–122;
  difference from existentialism, 6–
  7; difference from sick humor, 6;
  difference from surrealism, 7; difference from traditional comedy,
  7–9; exhaustion of guises of re-

ality, 23–40, 102; "Humor," x;
  literature of 1960's, 5; multiplicity
  of experience, 17–40, 43–45; non-
  moral stance, 9–13; parody, 66–
  69, 86–89; point of view, handling
  of, 21–23; protagonist, 12; *regressus in infinitum*, 23; skepticism,
  13–15, 61–64; unconfirmed thesis,
  43–51; undiagnosed illness, 23–24;
  unsensing of self, 51–55; vagueness of term, ix, 4–5; world as
  labyrinth, 17, 23–25
Blake, William, 62, 66, 89; *Europe*,
  xi; *Jerusalem*, 76
Böll, Heinrich: *Billiards at Half-past
  Nine*, 11, 131–132; *The Clown*, 11,
  13, 132–133
Borges, Jorge Luis, 6–7, 14, 22–23,
  29, 51, 61, 89; "Averroes' Search,"
  x; *The Book of Imaginary Beings*,
  19–20, 134–135; "Borges and I,"
  34; "The Circular Ruins," 82;
  "Death and the Compass," 70–71;
  "Everything and Nothing," 34; exhaustion of guises of reality, 23,
  29; "Funes Memorious," 27; "The
  Garden of Forking Paths," 70;
  With Norman Thomas di Giovanni, 19–20; With Margarita Guerre,
  19–20; "The Immortal," 40, 71;
  Labyrinths, 133–134; "The Library of Babel," x, 72; "A New
  Refutation of Time," 45, 105;
  Other Inquisitions 1937–1952, 134;
  parody, ix, 69–72; "Pierre Menard, Author of *The Quixote*," 71–
  72; "Tlön, Uqbar, Orbis Tertius,"
  69–70; "The Wall and the Books,"

153

36; world as labyrinth, 33–35; "A Yellow Rose," 67
Boyers, Robert, 27
Braine, John, 87
Brown, Charles Brockton: heroes, 115
Brown, Norman O., 27
Bruce, Lenny: sick humor, 6
Byron, Lord: *Don Juan*, 66–67

Cage, John: *Piece for Six Radios*, 53–54
Campbell, Joseph, 30
Camus, Albert: *The Stranger*, 6
Céline, Louis-Ferdinand, 3, 5, 10; *Journey to the End of the Night*, 8, 21–23, 25, 135–136
Cohen, Leonard, 72, 89; *Beautiful Losers*, 8, 26–27, 136–137; metaphysics of multiplicity, ix
Coleridge, Samuel Tayor, 62, 67; *The Rime of the Ancient Mariner*, 44; on Sir Walter Scott, 102, 106; on Waverley novel, 93
Comedy, traditional, 7–9
Comic apocalypse, see Black Humor
Conformist hero, see Black Humor
Conner, Bruce, 20
Coover, Robert, 22, 72, 89; parody, ix, 82–86; *Universal Baseball Association*, 13, 82–86, 137–138
Conrad, Joseph, 87
Custer, George: *My Life on the Plains*, 75

de Kooning, Willem: *Attic*, 53
Dippie, Brian W., 73
Donleavy, J. P., 3, 21; *The Ginger Man*, 6, 99, 104
Dostoevsky, Feodor, 11
Durrell, Lawrence, 5

Eliot, T.S., 61
Elkin, Stanley: *A Bad Man*, 87
Euripedes, 25
Exhaustion of guises of reality, see Black Humor
Existentialism, 6–7, 9; difference from, see Black Humor

Feiffer, Jules: sick humor, 6
Frank, Joseph, 102–103
Friedman, Bruce Jay, 7, 9–10; alienation of characters, 8–9; *Black Humor*, 3, 105; Black Humor, definition of, 3–5, 18; conformist heroes, ix, 97–100; *A Mother's Kisses*, 18, 24, 105–108, 139–140; *Scuba Duba*, 4; social violence, 114–119; Stern as conformist hero, 109–114; *Stern*, 8, 22–23, 97–100, 107, 138–139
Fromm, Erich: *Man for Himself*, 30; *The Sane Society*, 30
Frye, Northrop, 7, 12

Gallo, Frank: *Man with a Necktie*, 55
Galsworthy, John, 87
Glicksman, Hall, 20–21
Godwin, William, 8
Grass, Günter, 6–7, 72; *Dog Years*, 29; *The Tin Drum*, x, 8, 13–14, 18, 27, 29, 89, 140–141
Greene, Maxine, 52

Hair, 26
Hawkes, John, 5
Heller, Joseph, 3; *Catch-22*, 6, 13, 22–23, 25, 91–92, 95, 105, 141–142
Henry, Will: *No Survivors*, 75
"Humor," see Black Humor

Illness, undiagnosed, see Black Humor
Ionesco, Eugene, 6

James, Henry, 5
Johnson, Samuel, 66
Joseph, Gerhard, 35
Joyce, James, 87; *Ulysses*, 66–67
Judd, Donald, 21

Kaprow, Allan; Happenings, 101–102
Kermode, Frank, 104
Kienholz, Edward, 20, 103
Kiremidgian, G.D., 67–68